❦ ❦

The Living Body of Christ

DARTON · LONGMAN + TODD

First published in 2008 by
Darton, Longman and Todd Ltd
1 Spencer Court
140–142 Wandsworth High Street
London SW18 4JJ

Editorial Consultant: Jessica Rose

ISBN 10: 0–232–52718–0
ISBN 13: 978–0–232–52718–6

A catalogue record for this book is available from
the British Library.

Phototypeset by YHT Ltd, London
Printed and bound in Great Britain by
Athenaeum Press Ltd, Gateshead

CONTENTS

꽃 ꡳ

FOREWORD BY BISHOP BASIL OF
AMPHIPOLIS

❧ ❦

Metropolitan Anthony wrote very little, since he believed that the spoken word was the proper way in which to convey the truth of the Gospel. As a result, his books are almost entirely made up of transcriptions of talks and sermons he gave before live audiences.

This is true of the present collection of his reflections on the nature of the Church. Right from the start he makes it clear that, for him, the Church is something that can only be spoken of from within. With the Fathers, he accepts that even a prolonged catechumenate, however effective it may be, can never reveal to someone what the Church is really like. We need to be part of the incarnate Body of Christ, and to know the physical presence of other Christians, with all their problems, their failings, their sinfulness, and experience with them the physicality of the sacraments, in order to know the Incarnate Son of God in his fullness. The material world in its entirety belongs to the Church. Indeed the whole of creation cannot be grasped from God's point of view without the Church at its heart and as its end.

The effect of Metropolitan Anthony's own lived experience of the Church means that even dogma and doctrine come alive as he speaks. Theological discourse is 'speaking of God from within the knowledge of God'. The Gospel narratives, too, are brought to life as he speaks. They become three-dimensional scenes into which we are able to enter, and not just ways of teaching us things that we do not know. We are introduced to the direct, personal presence of Christ and invited to learn from him. All is real and based on experience, but an experience that is rooted in the prayer of the Church and the teaching of the Fathers. There is no trace here of what Metropolitan Anthony himself would sometimes call 'churchianity', where what is external has become so comfortable that it no longer reflects the often tragic power and dynamism of what is within.

Metropolitan Anthony was also extraordinarily open to the world outside the visible boundaries of the Church. The Church, he believes, is called to penetrate society like the working of leaven spreads through dough or fire through iron. At the same time he accepts that the 'outside' is also found within. The limits of the Body of Christ are permeable. In an extraordinary passage he says: 'Atheism – the loss of God that kills – is rampant outside the Church. It is also rampant within it to the extent that death has power over us.' The difference between Church and not-Church is not the difference between black and white, between good and evil.

The material in this collection covers a period of many years. Some of it reflects the conditions of the past. For example, he often speaks of the Russian Church as it was under communist rule, as a persecuted, weak body unable to preach openly the truth of the Gospel. This situation came to an end in 1991. His outlook also reflects very much the experience of exile, the experience of those who fled Russia in 1917 in the face of the violence of the Revolution. But he was one of those who, like Berdyaev, took exile as an opportunity for Christ and for the Church. The Lord of history had provided an opportunity to bring Eastern Christianity to the West.

Metropolitan Anthony was determined that Orthodox Christianity in the West should not suffer through its links with the State, as it had under the Tsars and then under the communists.

The Church should be free to be itself, the Body of Christ, an extension of the incarnation of Christ in the world. And like Christ, it should live in the knowledge that the Spirit of God rested upon it and filled it with divine life. Just as the Jewish diaspora in the Mediterranean basin and beyond prepared the way for Christianity and enabled the Church to transform the spiritual life of the Ancient World, so he hoped that an outward-looking, spiritually aware and confident Orthodoxy might contribute to the spiritual awakening and revitalisation of Christianity in the West.

Through his preaching and his talks Metropolitan Anthony sought to challenge his hearers to seek out Christ. In his person, many felt that Christ was seeking them. And it was only right that they should, for it is Christ who seeks to speak through the Church, through the individual voices of its members, his Body. Although Metropolitan Anthony spoke to all, to Orthodox Christians and non-Orthodox alike – and the message he proclaimed was received by all – it is the Orthodox who now bear the burden of taking up where he left off. We have yet to see whether his hope that Orthodoxy in the West will be free of the nationalism of the past and of the heavy hand of the State can be realised.

PART I

##

The Essential Church – a Living Experience

❧ ❦

The Church:
an Extension of the Incarnation

Today, when the divisions of the Church seem paramount in people's minds, it is good to be reminded of the deeper reality upon which all forms of authentic Christian community ultimately depend: the living Body of Christ, one throughout space and time, and one through its union with God and with the final destiny of the world. In this talk, given in Geneva in 1967, Metropolitan Anthony looks at this reality and relates it to the experience of every baptised Christian. He argues that it is only through experience that we can come to understand what the Church is. The French transcript appeared in the Messager de l'Exarchat du Patriarche russe en Europe occidentale, *109–112 (1982), pp. 25–35. It was translated by Benedict Roffey for publication in* Sourozh, 1992, No. 48, pp. 6–16.

How do we describe the Church?

I am going to speak of the Church only from one particular point of view, because 'the Church' is a vast subject which really includes all the problems of our faith. We live in the Church, and at the same time we wait for the Church to be fully revealed as the Kingdom of God. What I shall say about the Church will therefore be fragmentary, but it is, I think, essential for a more developed understanding of it.

When we speak of the Church we are prone to define it in terms which we take from our catechisms. All these descriptions are true, and yet they are insufficient if we wish to comprehend and know the Church. The reason for this is that the catechism, which is now studied by children who are already Christians, was originally intended for people who were not yet Christians; it was an introduction to the Church, and not a part of ecclesial life in its true depths. So what we find in it are definitions, explanations which are within reach of those who have not yet passed through the door leading into the Church, within reach of catechumens who are still outside the mysteries of the Liturgy, outside the prayer of the Church which is conscious of itself and offers – with Christ, to Christ and in the name of the living Christ – the articulated prayer of the created world. And thus these definitions, however true they may be, nevertheless leave us outside the Church.

They have the same sort of value as the explanations you might give to someone who comes to your city looking for a particular monument. You will describe it, you will try to make him feel the significance of it by stressing certain features that are peculiar to it; a sacred building will be defined by a certain number of characteristics which are not the same as those that you will choose for a town hall or barracks. But in spite of all that this may give you, such description does not lead you into the interior of the monument.

This is natural, because knowledge of the Church is above all an *experience* of the Church. Like everything that belongs to the divine realm, it is a knowledge made up of adoration, of communion, and of belonging. From this point of view, the Church appears to us as something very much deeper than a collection of definitions.

Yes, we are united by a single common faith, we possess the same sacraments, we serve the same liturgy, we have a hierarchy which unites us all and holds us together in a visible and perceptible unity. But the profound nature of the Church, the profound experience of the Church, is defined differently.

The Body of Christ: an extension of the Incarnation

Above all the Church is defined in the words of Saint Paul: the Church is the Body of Christ (Rom 7:4; 1 Cor 10:16; 1 Cor 12:27; Eph 4:12). This is an expression which is either so familiar to us that it has lost its meaning, or, on the contrary, so strange that it no longer offers us anything at all. It is a combination of words whose meaning we must rediscover from generation to generation, especially because the word 'body' has acquired over the centuries so many shades of meaning and has become, above all, a sociological reality: a trade association, an army corps, or a workers' union. These are terms which define a society whose nature is only that of a group of people united to face a common task or in a common situation. But when we speak of the 'Body of Christ', we speak of something much more real, much deeper than that; it is a term which is linked with the Incarnation, and not with the cohesion of members who might afterwards separate.

In what sense, then, can it be said that we are the Body of Christ? In the realistic sense, I believe, as was brought out by a Russian theologian of the last century, the Church is an extension of the Incarnation.[1] Each one of us is a *presence* of Christ, but in what sense are we an 'incarnation'? In what sense is Christ really present in us? Can we take seriously such expressions as that of Saint Paul: '... yet not I, but Christ liveth in me' (Gal 2:20)? If this is so, what remains of us, if Christ lives in me and I no longer live? What reality has this? Has Christ simply taken the place of the human person?

First of all, this definition of the Church as Body, as organism, helps us at once to understand that it is not a whole made up out of parts which are separable one from the other. It is a whole which is not made up of parts, but of *members,* and of members which are eternally inseparable from the moment when they unite in

---

[1] Cf. Ware, Timothy, *The Orthodox Church* (Penguin, London, 1993), pp. 241ff. for discussion of this idea and its exposition by Alexei Stepanovich Khomiakov (1804–60) in his well-known essay, 'The Church is One'.

a body. This feeling of an unbreakable unity was very strong in antiquity, and was expressed in a remarkable way by Justin Martyr.[2] Writing to one of his friends who had sinned gravely and was cut off from communion with the Church, he said: 'Do you not realise that as long as you remain outside this living body, the body of Christ has a wound which no one can heal but you?' The Church then, is not a matter of members who are interchangeable; one cannot forget a presence simply because one no longer perceives it; one cannot replace someone who was there by someone who was not there. Someone who belongs to this Body belongs to it in a way which may even be tragic, but he belongs to it for ever.

Baptism: death and resurrection in Christ

How does integration into this Body take place, and what does it mean? In the present practice of most Churches, one usually becomes a member of the Church as a child through the mystery of

[2] Christian apologist and martyr, c. 100–165.

baptism at such a tender age that although it is a mystical event, it is not a psychological event. It is not something which happens to us consciously, and therefore it is something that must be re-appropriated at a later stage so as to become a conscious reality. Without this re-appropriation baptism can be an event which is lost for years. When we think of the first generation of Christians, we see that baptism involved something else as well: a whole forward movement of faith which leads to integration in the Church, the Body of Christ. And this integration is precisely into the *person* of Christ. It is Christ who is central in what is happening.

We all know by experience the kind of deep identification which can take place between us and someone who is dear to us in moments of tragedy. Those of us who have lost someone whom they have loved above all others, whom they have loved profoundly, certainly know this experience. The death of someone who is dear to us seems to divide our life into two: the life which surrounds us with trivialities, which is unworthy of the event which has touched us so deeply, which involves events or circumstances that are not at the level of what has happened; and that which has the depth and the grandeur of life and death. There are moments – and these moments may, depending upon the depth of our feeling, last a few moments, a few days, months or, sometimes, a lifetime – when the death of someone carries off into the tomb all there was in us of futility, of vanity, of hollowness, all that has not the breadth, the grandeur of true human value. And it is something of this kind that is at the root of the experience which is the very foundation of baptism.

The word 'baptism' signifies 'immersion': to be baptised is to be plunged into the death of Christ and to return to life with a new life. This immersion in the death of Christ is something which is at once psychological, an object of personal experience, and an event in which God intervenes. At the level of the personal experience, of what is perceived, of what is conscious (or should afterwards become conscious), something happens which I would like to describe as follows.

You know that sometimes we are led into our deepest selves by a thought or by an emotion; something pulls at the very depth of our being, summoning all our powers. An inexpressible silence is created in us and we enter so far within ourselves that everything around us fades away, while something within becomes infinitely alive, intense and vibrant. When this involves our memories or our emotions, there comes a time when this inner state is broken. Gradually, or sometimes abruptly, we return to a consciousness of external things, and there remains only a memory, sometimes tinged with sadness, of that lost depth. There is in this image of baptism something analogous to our relationship to Christ.

If we enter into ourselves with the thought of the Lord, and if we go deeply into ourselves through faith, through love of Him who is our Saviour, in the depth of ourselves we meet Him. It is a personal meeting, living, concrete. It is not an image, it is not a memory, it is the Lord Himself. And that meeting nothing can destroy. We cannot be separated from the Lord: no power in heaven or earth can do it. It is like a kind of deep immersion in the presence of Christ, after which we return to our external life; but we are no longer the same.

What, essentially, has taken place on this level of the inner life, which is not yet that of the sacramental miracle of the Church? This meeting with Christ is a meeting with eternity, and when we return to our external life, it is not just in order to exist there, but to *live* there, enriched by the eternity which we bring back with us. When Christ appeared to the Apostles after the Resurrection, they themselves had in a sense died through the experience of His death on the Cross. He did not simply give back to them a new duration of earthly life: He gave them, within that earthly life, the presence of eternal life. This is the difference between the resurrection of Lazarus and the Apostles' return to life when they were bewildered and in despair after the Crucifixion. Lazarus was brought back from the tomb to live again until the moment when death would return him to the human condition; the Apostles returned to life without having been through physical death, but having taken part in a real death through their faith and their love for Christ.

The image I used earlier of a beloved person who carries with him to the grave all that is foreign to him, who seems to take from us all that is incompatible with him, is applicable here. Throughout His life, His communion of love with the Apostles, His teaching, His spiritual direction, the Lord had little by little separated everything in the world for them into what was in Him and around Him, and what belonged to the surrounding circle of hostility and the shadow of death. The death of Christ was for them not only the death of a Master, the death of a friend, it was the death of Him who possessed their life, who possessed the words of eternal life. His death was for them the extinction of life on earth, and what remained for them was simply to continue to exist. There could no longer be life for them, but only the duration of existence. The death of Christ had taken life itself from the world of the Apostles. It was not in vain that He had said: 'I am the Way, the Truth and the Life'. And the resurrection of Christ was not simply the joy of meeting with Him whom they loved, who was their master, their guide; nor was it the joy of a victory achieved when defeat seemed clear – it was a return to *life* in all its plenitude.

That is why the Apostle Paul, when he speaks of baptism in his Epistle to the Romans, draws a parallel between the death and resurrection of Christ on the one hand and, on the other, the immersion of someone being baptised into the waters of baptism with a view to their return to life.[3] These waters of baptism are a symbol: they

---

[3] 'Therefore we are buried with him by baptism into death: that like as Christ was raised up from the dead by the glory of the Father, even so we also should walk in newness of life' (Rom 6:4).

signify death. We plunge into them as if we were plunging into death, and we come out of them into life. But this image will itself remain dead if it is not rooted in the experience which I have just described. It is only a living image to the extent that there exists in us a living relationship with Christ. Without that relationship this death is an image, to be sure; but it is no longer a symbol, it is no longer something rigorously parallel to the event which it expresses. For the Apostles the death of Christ was their death, His resurrection – a new life. If this apostolic experience does not exist for us, if it is closed to us, we have not yet understood our own baptism.

There is also another side of baptism which is not simply psychological, but objective; and in spiritual life, the objective cannot do without the subjective. In the spiritual life the only objectivity is that which comes to life at the moment when it is known and lived personally. This is true of doctrine, and it is also true of the sacramental mysteries. And what takes place on God's part, on the side of the mystery, is a divine action which integrates us into the mystery of Christ. The act of faith and the act of love which must form the basis of the event itself make of us beings truly united to Christ in a way which is inseparable. This is a miracle, and in it God acts. Without this action there is no baptism; nor, without it, is there a Christian.

Our relationship with Christ

There we have an affirmation which I believe to be essential in the Orthodox understanding of the Church. The Church is essentially a sacramental body. It is not a society united by convention, even if this is the convention of faith. It is a society in which God acts and transforms, where God is active. Without the action of God, it is only a preparation which needs to be crowned, but which is not fulfilled.

So let us try to understand the relationship which exists between us and Christ in the case of a baptised Christian. There are two images in Scripture which I would like to use here. One is of the vine and the vine shoot;[4] the second is a phrase used by Saint Paul when he says that we, the pagans, are grafted onto the people of Israel. The pagans have been grafted on to the living olive tree, which is Israel, in order themselves to

---

[4] Cf. John 15.

become an olive branch full of life.[5] Let us try to see what are the implications of these images for our understanding of the Church.

First, the image of grafting. The gardener has a tree which is full of life, full of sap, capable of sharing and of giving life. He looks around for a shoot, a branch, a bush which is drooping, but which is still capable of being revived. This first action of the gardener, full of charity and of wisdom, is the searching which Christ has described, for example, in the Parable of the Lost Sheep (Luke 15:3–6). This is followed by an action which appears to be cruel and even violent in the experience both of the gardener and of the human person. The divine act of love which follows consists in pulling a branch from its roots, cutting it with a pruning knife, separating it from the life, transitory and ephemeral, which it none the less possessed, and suspending it in the possibility of total death. This happens when the gardener cuts with his pruning knife the branch he wishes to graft, but it happens also when, in human existence, the Master Gardener, the Lord, pulls one of us up by the roots, tears him away from his surroundings, from his

---

[5] Cf. Romans 11.

country, from his faith, from the conditions of his life, from all that was the support, the security of his life, sometimes from what was his very life itself; and holds him suspended between the death which awaits him and that transitory and ephemeral life to which he can no longer turn because he has been torn away from it by a violence which is divine.

And then the gardener turns towards the olive tree, to the tree he has chosen to give life, and once again he cuts, he cuts it open with his pruning knife, and it is in gash against gash, wound against wound, that the meeting between the life-giving olive and the dying branch takes place. And this also is a law of the spiritual life: it is only at the price of suffering, wound against wound, that the life of one being is transmitted to another. It is always at the price of suffering and at the price of a pouring out of life, a loss of life, that this meeting and this gift take place.

And now the branch finds itself grafted on to a trunk which can give it life. But does that mean that already the branch possesses life? What will happen? Did not the Lord say: 'If you abide in me, you will have life and bear much fruit' (John 15:4)? But how can the branch 'abide', when it has simply been placed there?

17

Now there begins a struggle which we can observe both in the graft and in the experience of human life. Slowly, insistently, the sap of the vine, or of the olive, presses forward, seeking to penetrate the tiny capillaries of the graft. It rises slowly, and penetrates them all. It reaches the last of them and surrounds each and every cell. Little by little it presses more firmly, more insistently, entering into the very life of each cell, displacing by its own life the wild, ephemeral life which led to death. And little by little the graft comes to live by a new life. Gradually its leaves unfold and it becomes alive in a more profound sense than before. But at the same time it becomes *itself*, in a more intense, more personal way than ever before. All its starved possibilities, which were unable to express themselves because they lacked life, flourish and come to perfection. And we see that the Lord was right when He said that if the graft abides in the vine, it begins to develop, to come to perfection and become itself in a way that we could not have suspected before.

Yes, it is the whole immensity of the infinite life of the life-giving tree which moves and informs the graft. And yet this graft is only itself because it has come alive with this fullness of life. And here we come again to the words of Saint

Paul: 'It is no longer I, but Christ who lives in me' (Gal 2:20). But Christ has not displaced my own personhood. I am still there; but all that I could be I have become, now that it is His life that is in me, His power to live, His eternal power. And the relationship of the Christian with Christ which we find in these images gives us at the same time both a fullness of personal life, and of shared life, since there is only *one* life – the life of God which is poured out in us.

And this life is not merely an earthly life which attains greater fullness, for He who gives us life is not just Jesus of Nazareth, the prophet of Galilee. It is He who is at once both man and God; it is He who is fully God, and it is He whose very humanity is not simply our humanity with an added divinity, but a humanity which has become again what it should have been without the Fall.

Saint Maximus the Confessor, speaking of the Incarnation, gives us an image for this. He tells us that the mystery of the Incarnation resembles what happens when a metal sword is put in burning coals. A heavy, cold, dull sword little by little becomes brilliant with light, and this light makes it appear to us brilliant and new. And the heat which fills it, this fire which fills it, means that we can no longer distinguish the heat and fire from the iron with which they have become integrated. As Saint Maximus says, we can burn with iron and we can cut with fire.[6]

There is in the mystery of Christ this inseparable union of His divinity and His humanity, which means that His very humanity surpasses itself and attains the real vocation of man, *theosis*, deification, the surpassing of the created in communion with the uncreated.

But what happens in Christ? Because in Him it is not a sword or fire we are facing, but a human person and a human substance united to God.

Saint Maximus reminds us that according to the teaching of the Bible and of St Paul, death is the result of sin, of the separation between us and God, and that the union of God with a human nature in Christ makes already of that human nature a nature that is immortal and incorruptible. Nevertheless, we see Christ suffer and die on the Cross according to His humanity.

This is because in an act of compassion, an act of love which accepts the total destiny of the beloved being in all its consequences, Christ accepts in His humanity (which itself is no longer

---

[6] *Difficulty* 5 (MPG 1060A), quoted in Louth, A., *Maximus the Confessor* (London & New York: Routledge, 1996), p. 178.

subject to either suffering or death) all the consequences of our fallen state and of sin. And yet, behind this vision of the suffering Christ, of a God infinitely weak and vulnerable who is delivered into the hands of men to do with Him whatever they want, there is the mystery of the victory already won, there is the revelation of Man in all his glory.

We see Him on the Mount of the Transfiguration, in His glory. But it is not He who has changed, it is the Apostles who are now able to see Him as he is. We see Him later at His Resurrection. Yet it is not His humanity which has changed, but that which was previously invisible, what God previously wished to hide, He now fully reveals. And it is into this glorious humanity, which is already that of the age to come, that we are integrated in the mystery of Baptism, if we truly die with Him and if truly we are reborn with Him.

Divine action and human response

I say 'if truly' not because the divine action is insufficient, but because our salvation is not a unilateral divine act, but an act of co-operation in which our human will and our human liberty fully take part. One of the Fathers of the Church said: 'God created us by his will alone, but he can only save us if we agree'. This is why it is not the fullness of the glory which appears in us on the day of our baptism, but a preliminary pledge of eternal life. In the words of Saint Paul, 'I can do all things through Christ which strengtheneth me' (Phil 4:13). It is a beginning, but at the same time it is an eschatological event in the full meaning of that word, for the word *eschaton* means two things: a decisive event and a final event. The decisive event has taken place: we have been grafted into Christ. The final event will be the fullness which is to come. In the same way the Incarnation, Christ's death on the Cross and His Resurrection are decisive events for the salvation of each of us, but in their final form they must be acquired, they must become a personal reality for us all.

As a result of this relationship it is truly, as the Scriptures say, a new people, a very special nation, which is born of the baptismal waters, of these waters which seem to be the primordial waters from which all things came according to the first chapter of Genesis: a re-creation, a new creature. Yes, a new creature, a new society, but more than a society, a living organism, the 'total man'. This expression of Saint Ignatius of Antioch has been frequently taken up by Saint Augustine: the total man, head and members – Jesus and all who are in Him with Him.

This total man is thus in a special relationship not only with Christ, but with the Holy Spirit and with the Father. The Scriptures, the experience of the Church, the meagre human experience we have been granted, teach us that no one can recognise the Incarnate God in the prophet of Galilee, in the man of Nazareth, in the criminal nailed to the Cross at Golgotha, unless the Holy Spirit itself reveals this to him. Someone who has believed, who has recognised Christ, who has responded to His appeal, who has entered into this mysterious communion with the mystical Body, with the body of Christ, has done so at each step by the action of the Holy Spirit.

This Holy Spirit first calls us, then teaches us, then integrates us, finally going even deeper. For when we have become the living body of Christ, the living presence of Christ through the ages and through earthly space from generation to generation, then in our depths He causes us to take part in a new experience, for it is He who teaches us to say 'Abba, Father' while addressing Him who is the Father of Jesus Christ in all eternity (cf. Gal 4:6). 'Abba' is a familiar name and the word 'father' translates it in a forced and solemn way. In the time of Christ, a child said 'Abba' to his father as in our time he would say 'Papa', or 'Daddy'. There is something profoundly moving and infinitely simple in this call of the Spirit from the depths of our soul.

What, then, is this call? Does the Spirit of Christ, which is the spirit of sonship, place us simply in a situation analogous to that of Christ? Here we meet one of the great affirmations of the patristic thought of the second century, a thought which frightens us by its boldness and comes to us from Saint Irenaeus of Lyons, who tells us that 'if all we believe of Christ and of the Church is true, then through the Church we are all together the only Son of God'.

How are we to understand this? We say often the 'Our Father', and this prayer is repeated not only by Christians, but by innumerable believers throughout the world. What, then, is there in this prayer? For some, it is an analogy, but for others it is a reality which would be terrifying if this reality were not God's love. The analogy is simple: if we know God in His works, in our experience as someone who acts as Father in respect of us, it is easy to call Him by this name. But for the Christian there is something else in this expression. For no one knows the Father but the Son and those to whom, if He wishes, the Son reveals Him. Nor does anyone know the Son but the Father, as the Gospel of Saint Matthew says (Matt 11:27). This knowledge is an experience which surpasses all analogy and belongs to the order of ontology, to the substantial reality of things. If in our love of Christ, and in the action of the Holy Spirit and of Christ in His sacraments, we have truly become the living body which Saint Paul says we are, then truly, with Christ, we have for our Father the Living God. This is our vocation. It is not simply something which is given to us mechanically, automatically, in the mystery of baptism, in the gift of the Holy Spirit, at Pentecost, in eucharistic communion. It is something which is given – and is either received or not received. Because the human response is as decisive as is God's gift. Grafted onto the life-giving plant, we share and have our part in the mysterious life of that divine eternity in sacramental communion, in the mystery of prayer, in the profound unity which establishes itself when we and Christ are united by the same will and the same life. And in that union the Father becomes *our* Father.

The meeting place between God and his creatures

Thus the Church is revealed to us as something much more profound and much greater than any human society, whatever its character. The Church is revealed as the mystery of the meeting and the union between God, One in the Holy Trinity, and His creatures, whose dispersion, whose division is overcome and whose unity is realised anew, first in an act of faith and then in a mystery of communion. The Church is the presence of the Most Holy Trinity in the midst of us and in us. It is the action of the life-giving Trinity in His creatures.

But the Church is not only glory. There is in the Church a poor and unhappy side; there is a glorious side and there is a tragic side. The poor and miserable side is ourselves; it is the empirical Church, the one that we see. It is not of her that we speak when we say: 'I believe in One, Holy, Catholic and Apostolic Church'. It is not in this empirical aspect by itself that we profess our faith, for that is what is visible – all too visible. In a certain sense we belong both to the world and, at the same time, already to the Church. As Father George Florovsky said, we are at once *in patria* and *in via*; we are already in the Church and we are on the way to enter it. So long as evil, sin and death are not yet vanquished in us, we are still in the process of transformation. But nevertheless, in a deeper sense, we are already the children of God; we are the companions of God in his work of salvation. We are like the crew of a lifeboat: we know the will of God, we have been called to be the companions of His labours. He has told us that He no longer wants to call us servants, but friends; for the servant does not know what his master wants, whereas to us He has told all that He wants. And in this there is a mysterious glory, a radiance, a light.

And then there is a tragic side. Briefly, it is this: Saint Paul says in his Epistle to the Colossians that we are like a colony of heaven on the earth; we are the representatives of a celestial metropolis in a strange land.[7] And in spite of this, we still claim that we are citizens of this land; faced with kings and those who guide and

---

[7] Cf. 1 Cor 15:47–50.

possess the nations, we claim to be both totally integrated in earthly reality and to represent a reality which surpasses it. It is not surprising, therefore, that the world rejects us and that we appear to it as a sort of 'fifth column', as traitors who pretend to be citizens of this world while recognising the power of a king who is not of this world; as a group of people for whom the only law is the act of love, while they remain estranged from the law of the land. And this law of love is a danger and a threat to the land, because love implies renunciation of self even to the point of death. And also because to be in communion with Christ, to have with Him a common life, means accepting the totality of His destiny, not only the glory which for us is yet to come, the eternal joy which for us is yet to come, but also His destiny in history: 'I send you forth as lambs among wolves ...' (Luke 10:3).

But this would be a new theme and a new subject. What I wanted to do was to show you the link which exists between Christ and the Christian and the unity of life which exists between all Christians, for it is the one Christ who is our life. Also the mystery of the Trinity – Father, Son and Holy Spirit – as it relates to that situation which we call the Church. And finally, the paradox of the Church, both already at hand and not yet here, present yet still to come. And the tragedy of the Church, because as long as the whole world is not saved, the mission of the Body of Christ remains the same: a body broken for the remission of sins.

❦ ❦

2

The Only Revelation of God

In this talk, given to the Kensington Council of Churches on 17 November 1986, Metropolitan Anthony begins from the idea of the Church as the place where God can find a home in this world, and shows how at the same time the Church reveals God to us.

God's home in this world

First of all I am not going to start with the well-known quotations which we find in the Scripture concerning the Church as being the Body of Christ (e.g. 1 Cor 12:27), the Pillar of the Truth (1 Tim 3:15) and so forth, although these notions will come within my talk. I would like to begin by saying a few words about the meaning of the word 'church' and the assocations it has with the old Israel. The word 'church', *kirk, Kirche*, comes from the Greek, *kyriakon*. It is the *kyriakon doma*, the house of the Lord. It is the realm of God where He is not only supreme but where He is at home. It is his place among men, not only because He has got power and rights, but because He is received and He is accepted by a congregation, by people who give themselves to Him unreservedly so that He can reign supreme and be the life of the Body.

The other expression which we find is the Greek *ekklesia*, which is a term taken from ancient Greek civilisation and which has given us the French word *église*. The *ekklesia* in ancient Greece was the assembly of all the citizens of a city possessed of full rights of citizenship, those people who had a right to speak and a right collectively to define the destiny of the city or of the city state.

These are the two elements which we find linguistically in the notion of the Church. It does not mean that the Church is a purely democratic body in which all its members are to make decisions according to their mind or their preferences. What is characteristic of the Church, what is unique in the Churches is the fact that the Church is the Body of Christ, and the life of the

Church, the mind of the Church in its entirety, is the mind of Christ. So that every single member of the Church aims at living, at being, such that they may say, 'It is not I but Christ who lives in me' (Gal 2:20).

The Church is there not only to express the collective mind of the people, but collectively to express and proclaim the mind of Christ, the mind of God. It is a prophetic body. A prophet is one to whom God discloses his thoughts, and this is one of the essential features of the Church.

On the other hand when we think of the Church as being the realm of God, we may well ask ourselves: how does it relate to the old Israel, which was God's own people? And I think we can find an explanation to this and a very stern warning to us about it in two passages from the Scriptures. Originally, after the covenant was established between Abraham and God, and through Abraham with all his descendants, Israel was God's own home and God's own people.

And we can see in the life of the patriarchs, in the life of the judges, in the life of the prophets, that God was the leader and the guide of the Church. He was unreservedly the Lord. He was unreservedly Him whose will was the absolute, unreserved law. But this kind of theocracy, humanly speaking, presented a problem to the people, because conveying the will of God was dependent on the presence within the people of God, of prophets, of saints, of people who could hear and could speak for God.

And in that sense, humanly speaking again – and I insist on this element – there was always a theoretical risk. What if in our generation no one shall hear? What if in our generation there will not be a prophet or one to whom the mind of God is open and who can proclaim it? And this came to a head in the time of Samuel. When the people saw that around Samuel were sons that were not prospective prophets, who were not proclaimers of the will of God, they turned to Samuel and said, 'We want to be like every other nation and be guided by a king', the implication being that it was too risky to hope that God would find someone to proclaim His will in every generation.[8] We want, they said, the security, the safety of human guidance and an institution that will make us secure, sure of today and sure of tomorrow. Samuel turned to the Lord in prayer. And the Lord said to him: 'Do not grieve, Samuel; it is not you, it is Me whom they have

---

[8] Cf. 1 Sam 8.

rejected. Give them a king, but warn them that this king – and I put it in abbreviated form – will be a taskmaster, will be an overlord. He will take their young men to be his soldiers. He will take their girls to be his concubines. He will rule them with a rod of iron, no longer like the shepherd of Israel which God was, no longer unto salvation, but to make of them a kingdom as vigorous and as unassailable as the pagan kingdoms that surround them.' In other words, there would indeed be earthly security but a very thin link with heaven, because within this kingdom there would be prophets, there would be saints, but they would clash with the institutions instead of being the guides of a people where there was no institution but all the flexibility of obedience to the divine will. And they continued in this ambiguous situation in which, on the one hand, the people of Israel were a nation like every other nation – they had accepted to a certain extent to become pagan – and yet they were still open to God by intention and by individual, personal obedience. And God spoke to them, because it was in Israel that the Messiah, the Saviour of the world, was to be born.

The second turning point, the decisive one that made Israel into something quite different even from this pagan and yet religious body, was in the days of Christ, when Pilate brought the Lord Jesus Christ out of the Pretorium and said 'Here is your king'. And the answer from the people of Jerusalem was 'We have no king but Caesar' (John 19:14–15). This was a last and final rejection of the leadership, the unique, total leadership of God. From that moment on it was another body that was to become the dwelling-place of God, the *kyriakon doma*, the House of God, the realm of God; a newborn body which was to be born of faith and of the Blood of the Lamb. At that moment the Church was ready to be born to replace the old Israel that had fallen away from its vocation and no longer was the home of God on earth.

Now when we think of the Church as we know it in the New Testament, we see a body of people, where every member who enters into this mysterious body does so by an act of personal faith and personal integration into it. It was not a body into which one could be born in the way in which one was born an Israelite. It was a body which increased in numbers because each one of its members chose to owe allegiance to no one but God in Christ. This is an extremely important thing. The Church is not a body to which one can belong by right. It is a body which one joins by choice, by surrender to God, by the gift of self to God and by the acceptance of God, of this allegiance. Faith is the link. The act that brings us to Baptism is ours. But it is Baptism and it is the grace of God given to us that integrates us to this body. This body is connected with God in ways which I will try to define.

First of all, however, I would like to say that one can give descriptions of the outer characteristics of the Church, but none of these descriptions will express the essence of it. If you turn to an Orthodox catechism you will be told that the Church is a body which is kept as one, is knit together, by a common faith in the Lord Jesus Christ and in all His teachings, in a common life rooted in faith and sacrament, in a hierarchy – not a hierarchy of power but a hierarchy of service, of people whom God has appointed to be shepherds of the flock and who are called to lay down their lives for others. But these are outer signs and one cannot, strictly speaking, recognise the Church in its essence by these signs any more than one can know what happens within a church or a cathedral by being told that such a cathedral is built in such and such a way. Even if you walk into it and see all its furnishings, all its images, everything in it, there is a mysterious life within it which is known only to the worshippers and to those who belong to that particular act of worship.

A divine and human body

And so one has to ask oneself: what is this body in an essential way? One could give as a definition of the Church the following: The Church is a body which is simultaneously and equally human and divine. It is not only a place indwelt by God. It is a place – and by place I mean people and not just the building – pervaded by this presence. When we speak of the building, of the church, of the cathedral, yes, it is the place of God. And indeed when you go to certain countries, to countries where there is persecution, or even to our own Western countries that have become so deeply secularised that in the street God is an alien, we can say the Church is His place of asylum. It is the only place which human faith has carved out of a world betrayed to secularity, betrayed to the power of Satan, and where God can rest assured that He is welcome, that this place is a place of safety for Him. And this place of safety is made possible by both the original faith and the continued, unshakeable faithfulness of the believers, ready for the sake of God, to give, to lay down, their lives. But the Church is not made of buildings. The Church of God is made of people. It is the Body of Christ. And what does this mean? It means that the first Member of the Church, the first person who united heaven and earth, in whom the fullness of humanity and the fullness of divinity are revealed, is the Lord Jesus Christ. And it is by being grafted onto Him, by sharing with Him both His humanity and His divinity, to whatever degree we are capable of sharing it, that we become members of the Church.

In Christ, the firstborn from the dead, the only man who ever has been truly Man – because to be truly Man means to be inseparably and perfectly united with God – in Christ we have a double revelation, a revelation of God and a revelation of Man.

The revelation of God is that which no one could have fathomed before – God who had been known as the great God of heaven, the Holy One of Israel, unattainable, unknowable, awe-inspiring, a terror to those who met Him even in longing – this God had become immanent, present among people, had chosen to be vulnerable, had chosen to become in the flesh one of us, helpless, given, surrendered to us. And yet, while He was immanent to the creation which He had brought into being, He remained a transcendent God, unknowable because He was the Son of God. In this union between Man and God, humanity, with all its possibilities, all its greatness, all its depth, was revealed. In the Incarnation we discover that Man is so deep, so great, so vast that he can be united with God Himself without being destroyed, without being annihilated, without ceasing to be truly human. Christ glows with the fullness of divinity, but it is His humanity which is aglow with it.

When we are grafted onto Christ by this act of faith which allows us to ask to be cut off from our human ephemeral earthly roots, to accept the risk of death in order to live – then we become partakers of what Christ is, both in His humanity and in His divinity.

And in the Church there are these two elements. There is Christ, who is the revelation of the perfect man. There are saints who are approximations to this perfection. In the Orthodox faith, as in Roman Catholicism, the Mother of God has already achieved this fullness of humanity. And then the saints of God, to differing degrees have come closer and closer to this fullness. So that we see the fullness of humanity revealed in the Church. But also we must remember that we are members of the Church, bringing into it our sinfulness, our imperfection, our frailty: we are in the making. And 'in the making' means that we are not yet perfect, not yet fulfilled. We are on the way, although we are already at home. We are already at home because we have by faith chosen God to be our Lord and no one else. We have surrendered to Him to the extent to which each of us could, as perfectly and imperfectly as each one of us can. And in that sense our relationship with God is already there, secure, because He has accepted us and He is our Lord, He is our God – He is our life, the life-giving Tree on whom we are grafted. At the same time, as the twig, grafted on the tree, is penetrated only gradually by the sap, we also have a degree of imperfection. And this finds expression in various ways. It finds expression in the imperfection of our knowledge of God, in the way we can speak of God, or reveal Him to others. St Paul says that we carry the holy things in earthen vessels (2 Cor 4:7). Yes, we are earthen and yet within us there is the fullness of our calling and the fullness of our surrender to God.

There is in the Church, then, a sort of double presence of humanity: the fulfilled, perfect, glorious humanity of Christ, true man and the Son of Man, and our imperfect humanity with all its consequences. But Christ is also God. And through Him the fullness of God resides within the Church. And not only through Him, because He sent us the Holy Spirit, who proceeds from the Father and was given to us by Him because we are at one with Him. We see the gift of the Holy Spirit bestowed and fulfilled in every human member of the Church in the mystery of Pentecost. The Holy Spirit is at work. He is fully there in the Church. He is struggling with us to conquer us and to teach us to be what Christ expects us to be. The Lord says that the Holy Spirit will teach us what He has taught, reveal to us the meaning of His teaching, guide us into all truth. He is the Spirit of Truth within the Church and He is the One who leads us into that communion with Christ and with Himself. And in Christ and in the Spirit we become the sons and daughters of the Most High. In the daring words of St Irenaeus of Lyons: by the power of the Holy Spirit we are called in the end of time to be the only-begotten son of God in the Only-begotten Son of God, being so one with the Son of God become the Son of Man that everything which is true of Him, even in relation to the Father, will become our situation with regard to God. So the Church contains the presence of God, contains the fullness of the Godhead in Christ, the fullness of the divinity of the Spirit and the fullness of the presence of the Father. And the Church also reveals to us the fullness of humanity in the Lord Jesus Christ. We Orthodox believe in the Mother of God and – to different degrees of perfection and glory, of resplendency – in the saints of God. But none of those who have surrendered to God, who have given themselves to God, however their lives are made up of ups and downs, of success and failure, of perfection and imperfection, can fall out of this relationship with God because it is founded, rooted in His love for us.

Becoming part of the glorious vesture of God

And so the Church is indeed a divine and human body. It is indeed a body in which we are confronted with God and in His presence. But to what degree, to what extent? In the Old Testament the people of Israel were God's own. They were linked to Him with a covenant, which meant a system of mutual obligations. They had to be faithful to His commands. They had to be obedient to His will. They had to be the witnesses of the Living God, and yet neither collectively nor individually could they enter into communion with God. We so often meet this phrase in the Old Testament, spoken by one saint or another, one leader of Israel or another: 'Woe unto me; I have seen God; I must die', because no one could approach God and remain alive, because God was the all-consuming fire. There was no access to Him. There was no way in which one could ascend from the earth into the divine realm of heaven. With the coming of Christ to earth it is God who came down to earth. It is God who took His place in our midst. And it is not a blasphemous thought of ours that we can be akin to God, because in His humanity He is one of us, and through baptism, by pouring His life into us, He makes us His brothers, His sisters. And He becomes at one with us, through the grafting, through the indwelling of the Holy Spirit, through our acceptance by the Father as sons and daughters of the Most High. We enter into a relationship with God that could not be fathomed in the Old Testament. We are at one with Him. We are pervaded with His presence. We are called – not only to be His people in terms of obedience and loyalty; we are called to become, as St Peter says, partakers of the divine nature (2 Pet 1:4).

This is our vocation. This is the degree of closeness which is open to us. And the Church is the place where we can meet God on these terms. It is the way in which God unites Himself to us and integrates us to His mystery. It is the very mystery of this communion with God through faith, through surrender and through His response of love, of sacrifice.

Yes, we are something of immense importance to the world. We are, throughout all ages, throughout space and throughout time, an extension of the incarnate presence of the Lord Jesus Christ, because we carry within ourselves His deadness, because we are called to be alien to everything which is alien to God. And at the same time we carry within ourselves the presence of Christ, the presence of the Spirit. We are what Christ was – not to perfection, but to a sufficient degree, like a spark, like a very quiet light and not like the light of noonday, but we are this presence, we are a continuous incarnation.

Bishop Mervin Stockwood[9] a number of years ago asked Patriarch Alexis[10] [of Moscow and All Russia] how he would define the Church. And the Patriarch said: 'The Church is the Body of Christ broken throughout the ages for the salvation of the world.' Christ died once and won a final and decisive victory, but throughout the ages He has in our persons witnesses who speak the truth as the Holy Spirit teaches them and who give their lives and their death as Christ did. In their bodies and in their souls it is Christ's life and Christ's death which is manifested and which reaches people unto salvation. So this is what we are called to be. And when we are told that the Church is the pillar and the column of the truth, yes it is, because the Spirit of Truth lives in it and because the one who is the true witness, the Lord Jesus Christ, lives in it – not only through us, but personally, because the ascended Christ is present in our midst, transforming, transfiguring this world. And when I speak of transfiguring, transforming this world, I should add one word about, not human history alone, but the world in which we live. The

---

[9] Bishop Mervyn Stockwood (1913–95), Anglican Bishop of Southwark 1959–80.
[10] Patriarch Alexis I (Simansky, 1877–1970).

Incarnation does not only mean becoming Man. We are not only told that the Son of God became the Son of Man. We are told that the Word, the Divine Word, took flesh, and the Body of the Incarnation is akin to all the created world, to all the materiality of this world, which is sinless, which is the victim of human sin. You remember the words of St Paul: the whole creation is groaning, waiting for the revelation of the sons of God (Rom 8:26). The creation is a victim of our sin. In the words of St Theodore the Studite,[11] the created world has gone mad, wild, anarchical: it is like a good, honest, genuine horse which is being ridden by a drunken rider. We are the drunken rider that drives this poor horse, which is the creation of God, into the madness which it endures and which rebounds on us. And it is the whole world that can look at Christ and recognise in Him its own redemption, its own fulfilment and the beginning of the glorious day when, having won finally His victory over all evil, all sin, all human resistance, God shall be all in all. And then indeed the whole of mankind will, in the Spirit and the Only-begotten Son, have become the only-begotten

---

[11] Theodore the Studite (759-826): abbot and monastic reformer who stood out against the iconoclasts.

son of God. And the whole creation will have become the glorious garment of God, a garment which is pervaded with His presence and which is a revelation of His glory. This is the Church in which we believe, not the institution which is such a temptation to all of us, but the essence of it. And we must learn, all of us, each of us, and make it possible for others to discover that yes indeed we are, personally through our sinfulness and unworthiness, our blindness, our sins, our inability to be what we are called to be – we are a screen between things divine and God. And at the same time the Church is the only thing that can reveal God.

I will end by telling you a story. We had in Paris a very remarkable theologian who was a doctor of theology. He was a most wonderful theologian, he could teach divinely. He had only one drawback. He drank desperately. And I remember someone, after one of his best lectures, saying to him: Mr So-and-so, how is it that you can show us the way to heaven and you remain rooted on the spot? How can you explain that? And he looked at his interlocutor and said, 'For you to find the way. What would you do if all the milestones began to run to their goal and left you to find your way alone?'

❦

3

The Church in Which We Believe and the Church in Which We Live

In this talk, given in London in 1978, Metropolitan Anthony explores the meaning and purpose of the Church in the world and the way in which its members represent the spirit of the Gospel.

The Church: a continuous stream of life

The subject of my talk is 'The Church in which we believe and the Church in which we live'. I will try to present the first as clearly as possible, speaking of the way in which we have an experience of the Church in our day-to-day life, and then try to link the two together. Those of you who have read Fr Georges Florovsky's article 'The Church: Her Nature and Task',[12] will know something which must be stressed: never has the Church given a definition of its nature. You will not find it in the Scriptures, or in the Fathers, you will not find it in any of the main statements like the Creed. What we find in the Scriptures is a very rich imagery that conveys an experience concerning the Church. In the Fathers we find very important commentaries on the credal and scriptural formulations, but they are given in terms of imagery, of analogy, or else they are drawn from the direct experience of members of the Church.

Even the best definitions fall short of telling us what the Church is actually about. If you take the Russian catechism of Metropolitan Philaret of Moscow, which is one of the finest catechisms we possess,[13] you will be told that the Church is a

---

[12] 'The Church: Her Nature and Task' appeared in volume 1 of *The Universal Church in God's Design* (SCM Press, 1948). Fr Georges Florovsky (1893-1979) was forced to leave Russia in 1920. An eminent writer and theologian, he taught at the St Sergius Institute in Paris, and later at St Vladimir's Seminary, New York, and Harvard Divinity School.

[13] Metropolitan Philaret of Moscow (1782-1867) was the first to have the Bible translated into Russian. He also wrote a catechism, published in 1823, which has remained a standard text of the Russian Orthodox Church. It was translated into English by R. W. Blakemore in his *Doctrine of the Russian Church*, Aberdeen, 1845.

body of believers who believe in the Lord Jesus Christ, who are united with one another by the Community of the Faith, of the Sacraments and of Hierarchy. Yet, unless you are introduced into the mysterious life of faith, of liturgy, of sacrament, of spirituality, which goes on within it, you would not be any more advanced by knowing this than you were before.

Equally forcibly Fr Georges Florovsky underlines the fact that every epoch in the history of Christendom had to wrestle with the life of the Church, the consciousness of the Church, the knowledge of the Church – about God, about Man, about the Church itself – from different angles and at different levels. The early centuries proclaimed and declared with final beauty and perfection the teaching which we now possess concerning the Holy Trinity, concerning Christ and the Mother of God. Our century, and recent centuries of crisis within the life of the Church, seem to be a time in which we have to wrestle with the problem of the Church – what is the Church, what is its nature, what are its limits, what is it that makes us members of it? In a very simplified way one may answer that the Church is about you, believers who proclaim the orthodox faith – orthodox with a small 'o', not a capital 'O' – the truth of the Gospel in its interpretation and its perfection. It is where the sacraments, mighty, wonderful acts of God take place: saving, transfiguring both Man and nature, where the life once given by the Holy Spirit pervades us, conquers us, and transforms us.

But a definition of this kind does not allow us to recognise in the diversity of Churches – that is, in the plurality of Christian confessions and denominations – the original and continuous stream of life which is the Church. On the other hand, at the other extreme there is a very simple way of approaching the problem by saying that the Church is a body which is canonically defined by its relation to something historically definable. It can be the See of Rome or it can be the canonical limits of the Orthodox Church, or the Baptist Alliance.

We cannot hope to evolve a definition which would be an earthly description of the nature and life of the Church. Rather than seeking for a definition, the Fathers tried to reveal and declare, proclaim and manifest the glorious reality of the Church. Our problem is not to find the right words that will encircle the notion of the Church, but the right way in which, being the Church living in all its fullness, we may reveal it. To use the words of St Paul, we must reveal it not in the words of wisdom of philosophers, but by the manifestation of the power of God within it (cf. Col 2). The power of God within the Church is not our power, it is the revelation of what God can do to us, can make of us singly and collectively, to reveal Himself and to reveal that a new time has come – that we are in a totally eschatological realm, a realm which is already now, within history, the presence, the immanence of eternity and of things final and ultimate. The Fathers did exactly this. They did not attempt to work out scholarly definitions but spoke of concrete situations from within the experience of the Gospel and of the Church in which they were rooted, which possessed them and held them within its power.

Experience of the Spirit

Now, let me turn to what the Church is in essence. In its deepest possible essence it is the experience which we all have incipiently, and which is possessed by the Church at large with a depth and a magnificence which has conquered nation after nation. The Church is not what it appears to be, a simple congregation of people who believe in God as revealed in Holy Scripture, who obey rules and follow the commandments of God, who share the sacraments, who are united by a common hierarchy, although all these things are part of the being of the Christian Community. The Church is an organism, a living body, which is simultaneously and equally human and divine. It is human in two different ways: it is human in us, and to us we will return when we speak of the frailty of the Church and of its problems. But it is also human in the person of the Lord Jesus Christ who is true man, and the only true man, because in Him man is manifested and revealed in all his greatness, in all his possibilities.

We are called to be what St Augustine called 'not only Christians, but Christ Himself' – the total Christ, head and members. The two, almost severed from one another, are united because Christ makes us one with Himself through those wonderful, mighty acts of God which we call the sacraments. In baptism, if we accept to be merged and identified with His death, we rise again in the fullness of the incipient, the germinate fullness of His eternal life; in the Eucharistic community we are united in Him in such a way that He is in us and we are in Him.

Angelus Silesius[14] said in one of his short poems 'I am as great as God. He is as small as I'. But it is not only through Christ and in Christ that the Godhead abides in the flesh, that God is present, integrated to human history and the life and being of the Church. God has also given us the Holy Spirit. Twice was the Holy Spirit given in two different ways. At the end of the Gospel according to St John, when Christ first appeared to His disciples, He breathed on them and said, 'Receive the Holy Spirit' (John 20:22). They received the Spirit because through mystical participation in Christ's death, they had become one with Him in such a way that the Spirit who had come upon Him on the banks of the Jordan, was now shared with His body – this extension of His bodily, incarnate presence – the twelve. This gift was not given to any of them separately, but to the apostolic band as a whole, as we can see from the fact that Thomas, who was not there on that evening, when he met the Lord Jesus Christ a week later at His second appearance to them, did not need to be given the Spirit separately.

---

[14] Angelus Silesius (1624–77): a German mystic of the counter-reformation.

The Spirit was, as it were, held in trust, possessed by the body to which he belonged, although he had been physically absent at the moment when the Lord had come and revealed Himself as the Risen Christ.

Then, at Pentecost, because of this body which was possessed in its entirety by the Holy Spirit, each member could be fulfilled in a personal, unrepeatable, unique way by the gift of the Holy Spirit which brought each person to perfection, to fulfilment. So God is present in the Church through this double gift of the Spirit given to the total Church, and the gift of the Spirit which each of us receives sacramentally in Chrismation and in the laying-on of hands. We become both the Church in its entirety, and each of us 'living temples of the Holy Spirit' (cf. 2 Cor 6:16), with the difference, however, that a temple made by human hands is made to contain, while we are pervaded. By the power of the Spirit which effects our oneness with Christ (because this oneness is fired and achieved by the act of the Spirit) we become with regard to the Father what Christ Himself is and the Holy Spirit teaches us to call God, the God of heaven, the Holy One of Israel, the unapproachable, transcendental God, with the name of Father. In Christ, by the power of the Spirit, and through Christ alone – there is no other way to the Fatherhood of God – we become sons and daughters of the Most High, brothers and sisters of Christ.

It is quite clear that all this is beyond human capabilities. No one can achieve this, no one can become what we are to be unless God gives it to us and we open ourselves to receive. It is through the sacraments that all this happens. They are not simply additional to it, they are the very core and essence of it. It is the waters of Baptism, the Chrism, the bread and wine of the Eucharist, all the acts of God that act with sovereignty when we open ourselves and say 'together with the Spirit, come Lord Jesus, and come soon', that these things can be effected.

The power of God is then truly made manifest in weakness, but not in slackness or sloth, not in the weakness of those who have neither courage nor faithfulness, but in that mysterious weakness which is transparency, perfect subtlety in the hand of God, and which can be compared to the sail on a boat, the frailest part of the boat but which when directed in the right way can engulf the wind, the spirit, and carry the boat to its destination.

When we think of the Church in these terms we can see that the Church is the very mystery of this union of God with His creatures. The Church is the place where all that takes place. This is why one can speak of the Church as both the people of God, and the City of God – the people of God in the sense in which I have spoken, and the City of God because it is a City, it is a body of people who are a society, which is greater than any society and city of the world because it is the place where God Himself dwells.

Experience of life in the Church; sickness and healing

For the outside world the Church is made manifest through us and we must by vocation mirror the mysteries of the divine society, of oneness in plurality, of oneness that transforms personal, limited being into a trans-personal beyond personal life and being. This was expressed in the early centuries by the so-called '34th Apostolic Canon' which tries to link the structure of the Church with the mystery of the Trinity.[15] The

[15] The 34th Apostolic Canon dates back to the beginning of fourth century and is probably an attempt to sum up the consciousness of the Church of an earlier time – which is why it is called 'Apostolic'. For a fuller discussion of the canon see Chapter 7.

sense of this canon is this: on a territory where there is a Metropolitan and several bishops ruling their dioceses, do not let the Metropolitan do anything otherwise than in unanimity with the junior bishops, and let no junior bishop do anything without the assent of the Metropolitan. It concludes, 'So shall God be made glorious: One in the Trinity.' This was the basis of the Church's consciousness of itself as a body whose rule is neither power nor organisation, but charity. Charity is the ability to cherish to the extent of laying down one's life for another, of living for the sake of others, of thinking only of the beloved, because the other, singly and as a body, will proclaim, assess, affirm us in all eternity. Gabriel Marcel says 'to tell a person "I love you" is tantamount to saying "You shall never die"', because it will be an assertion for ever of the ultimate beauty and significance of the person loved.[16]

On the other hand there is the empirical Church – the Church as we experience it. The empirical Church means all the history of Christendom, and all our private, personal and corporate history. Each one of us is unique, has a

---

[16] Gabriel Marcel (1889-1973): French philosopher, Christian existentialist and playwright.

unique relation to God and yet none of us singly is the Church. As the old saying went, 'A lone Christian is no Christian', because Christianity is oneness in Christ and in the spirit of people who are gradually becoming the total Christ, the Only Begotten Son, the new Adam. St Ephraim of Syria said, 'The Church is not the assembly of the righteous, the Church is a crowd of repenting sinners',[17] and the operative word is neither 'crowd' nor 'sinners', but 'repenting'. To repent does not mean bewailing one's misery: it means becoming aware of what sin is – separation from God, separation from one another, division within oneself, severance from the very root and depth of one's own self. Those who repent are those who have become aware of this and have understood that by no human effort can this be remedied and have turned Godwards. The word 'conversion' means turning around, and the Greek word '*metanoia*' means the same thing.

In what respect are we, according to St Peter's words, 'a peculiar nation' (1 Pet 2:9), a people that cannot be compared with any other? It is because however simple we are, however far from the ideal and the calling which is ours, we

---

[17] Ephraim the Syrian (c. 308–73): theologian and prolific hymnographer.

still possess as a seed, incipiently, but with the dynamic power of eternal life within us, that eternity which the whole world wants and expects in the future, but which is already in us and within us. In that sense we are eschatological persons and an eschatological body – a body which belongs to the kingdom to come that has been now implanted here through the Incarnation and its extension, the Church.

In that sense perhaps a phrase of C. S. Lewis describes very adequately both our vocation and what the Church is. He says, 'The difference between someone who has not met Christ and God, and received the Spirit, and one who is a member of the body of Christ is the same as that between a statue and a living person.'[18] A statue may be, and usually is, more beautiful and more impressive than most of us. Yet a statue is not alive and, says C. S. Lewis, 'the message of the Gospel is "behold the statues are coming to life".'

We do not have to be Michelangelo statues to be impressive if we come to life. Let us not think that we must become Michelangelo figures and then begin to move. Let us start by moving and we may later be revealed as Michelangelos.

---

[18] Cf. C. S. Lewis: *Beyond Personality*, Ch. 1. Geoffrey Bles, 1944.

The Church in which we live is thus a peculiar society in which something unheard of anywhere else is already happening. There is in it knowledge of God, communion with God, a presence of eternal life within us, that makes us truly, substantially children of the Most High. But it is also a very curious society in another respect. The Church is both profoundly sick and yet healing and life-giving. That is something of which we are all aware. Who would not say that he is surrounded by sin, and therefore sick in heart and mind? At the same time, because the Church is simultaneously and equally both human and divine, it can impart that life which we possess, to each of us, only to a very small degree perhaps, but it is a life which we can impart without measure because the Spirit is given by God without measure, and anyone who comes to us to become one of us sees grace and fulfilment greater than the one who gives it. Is it not obvious that all the Saints whom we venerate throughout the year were men and women who were baptised, anointed, instructed, given communion by priests who had not become saints? They received through the agency of those priests because it was not the priests who gave, but God who acted through them: the Saints became what the other could not achieve. St Seraphim was baptised by an ordinary parish priest and he is one of the glories of the Russian Church.[19] This body which is the Church is a body which we can believe in passionately as a body capable of giving life, of resurrecting the dead, of renewing and transfiguring, of transforming and starting new life.

As to ourselves, we might well be more tolerant with one another than we often are. An image for the Church which is far from scriptural, but which is modern and clear to most of us is that of Alcoholics Anonymous, which alcoholics join in order to support one another in their endeavour to be healed. They come to one another, they are not afraid of sharing with one another their condition because they are all in the same plight and therefore anyone who has made even slight progress can teach the others. We have, however, one sad characteristic which differentiates us from AA. Every alcoholic who joins the society knows that he is an alcoholic. Many of us are not sufficiently aware that we are sinners and therefore we are not in a search for healing in the way in which AA people are, and

[19] St Seraphim of Sarov (1759–1833): one of the best-loved Russian saints.

we are afraid of being recognised as sinners because we are in a society, in a group of people whom we do not trust to be aware and accepting, rather than to shrink away and reject us.

The Church is a curious society in another respect. It is a society in which one cannot be born, one does not belong to by birthright; one has to be re-integrated, grafted, included into it. It is impossible to enter it other than by the narrow gate of faith and sacrament. But it has also a characteristic which other societies do not have. It is a society in which membership cannot be retained if the inner condition for membership is not kept. There are certainly enough 'dead' members of the Church, people who were baptised at birth and who are eventually buried by the Church. In the interval they may have strayed into Church for their wedding or for the baptism of their children. But St Augustine firmly warns us, saying 'the time will come, at the Judgement, when many of those who thought they were within the Church will discover that they are alien to it. They possess none of its characteristics and many who thought they were outsiders will discover that they belong to it because they possess marvellously, wonderfully its characteristics.' To use St Paul's imagery 'the law of God was written in their hearts' and they followed it (Rom 2:15). It is not a question of canonical allegiance. It is not a question of being excommunicated or remaining in communion. It is something which God alone can judge, but God judges without error. He knows who is His own, and He knows who has fallen away from the dignity, the grace of his vocation. We must be aware of this, because the words of St Paul that one can receive communion 'unto condemnation' (1 Cor 11:34) may well apply to us who have lost the substance of the body of Christ and are only empty shells. The criterion is not righteousness, because otherwise St Ephraim the Syrian's definition would fall short of reality. The criterion is the way in which we relate to God as sinners, in repentance, in faith, in hope, in the exultation of a God so wonderful that salvation is ours if we only open ourselves to receive it. We are in that sense, in spite of our inadequacy, the realm of God, the *kyriakon*, the place where God is Lord undividedly.

Leaven in the world

The *kyriakon* or *ekklesia* was understood in the context of messianic preparation and fulfilment in the Old Testament, and therefore it implied a definite theology of the meaning of history and the workings of God within it. It also implied the understanding of a Greek city as an ultimate unity of citizens, of people conceived as a whole. Christendom is both the people and the city, but a city that is vast enough to be the city of God at the same time as a city of man. Christendom is incorporation into the Church, and not just into any ecclesiastic sovereign body, but into one particular body which is the Apostolic Church in the unity of faith and life with the Twelve at one with Christ.

I do not want to speak of the other aspects of the Church – the catholicity which means that the Church is for all and through all, the oneness which is its very nature, or the holiness which is not ours but God's within it.

The Church has manifested its life in different ways: first, the Church – the members of it – aware of its holiness and of its mysterious perfection has desired to create a society which is totally ruled by nothing but the divine will and has rejected all outside influences. This is what we find in the Desert Fathers, this we find in the early monasteries, people who left the world not because the world was wicked but because they thought that the Christian world had become weak, compromising, unsafe, had lost its integrity and absoluteness. Then we have another body of Christians who can be divided into quite different groups. One group was that of 'fair weather' Christians, after the conversion of the Emperor Constantine, when being a Christian was no longer dangerous, and Christianity had become the prevailing religion. Whether those people were truly Christians we cannot judge but weakness, compromise and slackness came very deep into the Church. Then there was a body of people who believed in the integrity of the Church but who also believed that the Church had been left on earth like a seed that had died in the ground in order to bear fruit, or like a handful of leaven, of yeast, thrown in the dough, that must disintegrate, become imperceptible in order to transform the dough. This can be illustrated by many examples throughout history.

Attempts have also been made, though unsuccessfully, to make of the Gospel, which is a call to a relationship, a legal system of relations.

The Court of Justinian attempted to make the ideal of the Gospel into law.[20] It was unsuccessful as far as achieving the building of a Christian world was concerned, because it transformed into a law what was the imponderable relationship, the mysterious way in which people have to relate both to God and to one another and to the Cosmos at large, which is present in the body of Incarnation, in the substance of the sacraments, in the possibility of the whole world to become an investiture of God. When we think of the world that surrounds us we must be very attentive not only to what happens within a given communion or within Christendom, but we must be aware of the fact that many of the things which the Gospel has brought into life have found their way outside it and are like leaven preparing the ground for the conversion of nations. The notion of the uniqueness of the person, the notion of the absolute value of people, the dignity of man, to take a few examples, are those of the Gospel, and we find them everywhere in what we would now call the modern pagan world. We must help and contribute to this world all that it can receive and

---

[20] Justinian I: Byzantine Emperor, 529–565. His *Code* systematised all the Imperial constitutions up to that time.

contain so that it may ripen gradually and become capable of this magnificent, glorious and resplendent reality which the Church is to be and which as long as history goes on will be in a twilight with saints that shine with all the glory of God and sinners that look Godwards and people in the making who are trying to find their way. What we are trying to do now, now in this small group of people which is our Diocese[21] is to become aware of the immeasurable divine power of God in the Church, which is capable of transforming us in the whole world if we only allow God to act through us so that one day Orthodoxy becomes here not one more denomination – this is of no interest – but a divine presence, a leaven, a power of transfiguration in this country and throughout the world.

---

[21] The Diocese of Sourozh, founded by Metropolitan Anthony in 1957. Until 2006 his followers remained within the Diocese, which is still part of the Moscow Patriarchate, but after his successor, Bishop Basil, was received into the Ecumenical Patriarchate in June 2006, many, feeling that the vision of Metropolitan Anthony was no longer being carried forward in the Diocese, left to form the Episcopal Vicariate of Great Britain and Ireland within the Archdiocese of Orthodox Parishes in Western Europe based in Paris.

PART II

✤ ✤

Heresy and Doubt

4

❦ ❦

The 'Onslaught of the Intellect' and the Potential of Doubt

The following is an edited version of the Lev Gillet Memorial Lecture 1987, first published in Sobornost *(journal of the Fellowship of St Alban and St Sergius), Vol. 9, No. 2 (1987), pp. 6–13.*

'That which we have seen with our eyes'

It is important to remember that the first generation of the Church's members knew Christ as a person, and some of them from very early days. Nazareth, Capernaum and Cana are little towns or villages distanced from one another by a few miles; it is not inconceivable that those who later became Christ's apostles and disciples had even met the Lord when he was a boy, a youth, a young man, and had thus discovered him in a

THE LIVING BODY OF CHRIST

gradual manner. In due course we can see disciples gathering around him, discovering in him a unique friend, a guide and an adviser, then a leader. Eventually they were to discover him as he truly was: as God who had come to them, who had come into the world.

This progress reaches the kind of culmination to which the words of Philip point early in the Gospel of St John: 'We have found him of whom Moses and the prophets did write, Jesus of Nazareth' (John 1:45). And what I said about its early stages may well explain the response of Nathaniel, 'Can anything good come out of Nazareth?' For if you were to be told that somebody you have known practically from childhood, an inhabitant of a small town round the corner from your village is declared to be the Messiah, the Saviour of the world, you would probably react in much the same way.

The first disciples had such a direct experience of Christ, and it was important for the world that the first witnesses should be people who had been with him from the beginning, had step by step discovered him for who he was. Indeed, when Judas died his tragic death and the disciples wanted to elect an apostle to take his place, they made it quite clear that they wanted someone who had been with them from the beginning and gone through this gradual process of discovery. Thus they could all speak directly of Christ's days in the flesh as the days in the flesh of the incarnate God.

'That which we have seen and heard declare we unto you'

The years passed, the apostles preached and proclaimed what they knew in the deepest and most personal way. Later – several decades later – the New Testament writings took shape. Fr Georges Florovsky once noted the importance of the fact that these scriptures were not produced as immediate, spontaneous, lyrical descriptions of what the disciples had undergone. Otherwise one could have doubted the validity of writings produced under the effect of strong emotion and deeply shaking events. Thirty, forty, sixty years later, these written testimonies appear as a mature reflection of people who had known Christ in the flesh, discovered the Christ of the Spirit and proclaimed an experience that could no longer be suspected of being merely an emotional response to friendship, love, bereavement or hallucination. Rather could it be seen as something deeply considered and true, not only autobiographically, but objectively. It could be seen as God's own truth about Christ.

With the passage of centuries these scriptures are received, are lived by, are experienced not only as the object of scholarship but as the means of communing in the experience which they convey. And not only they. To this day believers are able to assert, 'I know that God exists because I have met him'; 'I know that Christ is risen, because within my experience I know the living Christ'. It may be through prayer, it may be at moments of particular illumination, it may be through the sacraments. One way or another, it is a direct conviction.

But at the same time there was a watering down of the experience in the life of many. It is easy to understand that in the heroic times when the Church was persecuted, when to be a Christian was not only costly but entailed the risk of torture and death, only the few were Christians: those who were prepared on the ground of an experience they had lived, an experience which they could not deny without denying themselves. But when the Church was permitted to exist openly, and later became the Church of the

Empire, floods of people came into it who would never have thought of joining the Church when it was a question of life and death. This dilution of commitment gave rise to several different factors.

On the one hand monasticism was born as a reaction against the anaemic Christian society which was taking shape. It began as a protest not against the world, but against the Church which had become weak and unsure in many of its members. It involved an exodus away from the weaklings of the Church.

It was not an escape into the desert by people who were afraid of living in the city. It was a migration into the battlefield with Satan. It was an exodus of those who wanted to fight the true fight rather than live a comfortable life of devotion within the framework of religion while yet possessed of a secular world-outlook.

The 'onslaught of the intellect'

At that stage another phenomenon came to the fore. It was what Daniel-Rops[22] has called the 'great onslaught of the intellect'. The intellect

---

[22] Daniel-Rops: pseudonym of Henry Jules Charles Petiot (1901–65), Catholic writer.

marks the period of the Councils. People submit the faith to the criteria of their intellectual acceptance or rejection. Is it possible to believe this and that? Is it possible to accept such and such realities testified by the apostles and proclaimed by the Church? Can one reasonably be a Christian?

On the lowest level, it could have been seen that way. On a higher level, for instance that of Arius, the problem was more complex and more earnest.[23] For Arius was a man of great culture and of outstanding intelligence. And he submitted the Christian faith to the test of philosophical assessment. One may see that he is an outstanding example of what a heresy can be when the intellect is considered as empowered to judge revelation, to judge the formulations of those who possess an experience which the observer himself does not possess, either at all or to the same degree. For Arius, the problem was basically that God could not become man since an infinite God could never become the prisoner of finitude. God was eternal, and could not become the prisoner of time. And in those days (and I refer once again to Florovsky, since for me

---

[23] Arius (c. 250/256–336): condemned as a heretic by the Council of Nicea in 325.

his word has enormous value) no Arius could resolve the problem. Indeed, it took centuries of philosophical and scientific reflection and research to arrive at a vision of time which can accommodate the notion of eternity and space. For the first scientific book I know which really faces the problem (Emile Borel, *Le temps et l'espace*) was only written at the turn of the century. Before that, there was no scientific or philosophical basis that would allow someone to make the distinction and yet to realise that there is no contradiction in eternity pouring into time and not being a prisoner of it, or in infinity being within space and not being limited by it. Time and space, eternity and infinity were simply different categories.

One could say that eternity and infinity are God, and all the rest are created. But it is possible to go further. St Maximus the Confessor, speaking of the Incarnation, says that the divinity and the humanity in Christ are united to each other in the same way in which fire can pervade a sword plunged into a furnace. The sword enters the furnace cold and grey, without any brilliance; it emerges aglow with fire, resplendent. Fire remains fire, iron remains iron. But this is imagery that would not have satisfied

Arius: an image does not provide an answer to a philosophical question. Nevertheless this kind of image is an adequate description of a direct experience; and in this lies its importance.

What we find in this period of the Councils is people who try to address the Gospel proclaimed by the Church from the first days to their own time against the background of classical philosophy or of the various philosophies and mystery religions that had developed later. Some harm could have been done because some of the imagery could be compared with that of the Gospel and could thus be used as an accusation that the Gospel itself is simply a new mythology.

Doubts were engendered in the minds of many: is not Christianity simply a more elaborate and philosophically more acceptable myth, but still of the same kind (and as unreal) as the mythology of the various nations of the past? As philosophical thought developed, as philosophy taken from the ancient world acquired a new maturity, the intellect came to feel self-sufficient, no longer in need of being guided by God himself. Thus problems arose from the confrontation of a mature intellect with the problem of faith.

The nature of doubt

Perhaps I should say a few words about the nature of doubt in this context. If you consider that your intellect is the criterion and that you have a right to submit all the data of revelation and all forms of experience to the judgement of the intellect, you are bound to condemn as unacceptable everything that does not fit within the categories of your intellect at the point of development it has reached at a given moment, and in the context of the culture which is yours at this particular time. Yet this is exactly the phenomenon before us. No longer is it the experience of the Church which is the object of this onslaught of the intellect. It is the scriptural text itself which may be taken to be faulty when it does not correspond to the intellectual expectations of the reader. The text can be reinterpreted or misinterpreted in ways which can be warranted perhaps by linguistics. But this is to forget that language forms part of a spiritual tradition and must be understood within this tradition and not outside it. Not surprisingly, it becomes a commonplace to attack the text of the Gospels, to argue that it is unsatisfactory, that it must be understood in a way in which the Church never did understand it. Here, indeed, is something which is inherent to the human approach to truth, and at the root of any progress in thought or in experience.

Let me make a parallel between the doubt, or succession of doubts, which a believer can have, and the way in which a scientist confronts created reality. A scientist collects all the existing facts of which he is aware. To begin with they are disparate, and the scientist tries to group them, and at a certain moment, when a number of facts are capable of being held together, a model is built that allows him to hold all these facts together and reason about them in their totality. If the scientist is honest and creative, the first thing he will do is to ask himself whether his model holds, whether it is a model that has no intrinsic flaw within itself, whether it takes into account all the information possessed to date. If he is satisfied on these counts, his next move will be to look for new facts that will not fit in with his model and will explode it. For the aim of a scientist is not to create a model for which he will be remembered in the history of science. His aim is to create temporary models, hypotheses, models that *must* explode in order to enlarge knowledge and to contain new knowledge.

Doubt in that respect for a scientist is a creative activity, an activity which is elating because the discovery that something does not fit in a preconceived or ready-made model allows him to discover reality on a wider scale and to see that reality unfolds wider and wider, deeper and deeper, making it possible for him to discard one hypothesis after the other, one model after the other. For him reality is unshakeable and cannot be lost because the model is exploded.

What is tragic in the doubt which we find in a believer is that instead of saying that the model of God, of creation, of the Church, of man which satisfied him fifty years ago no longer satisfies him, can no longer satisfy his intellectual and spiritual development, he makes an either/or decision: either to retrench himself in the old or to abandon his former position altogether. Whereas the developing person who rejects the model he earlier had of God or the creation when confronted with the depths and range of science or of philosophy, is proceeding with something not only legitimate but essential. By contrast, a believer who at the age of eighteen or eighty would remain faithful to a model adequate for an eight-year-old would be spiritually and mentally backward, incapable of communing with all the vastness, depth and greatness of God and of his creation.

Doubt, creative and destructive

Doubt, then, is legitimate. It is creative, an important part of the discovery of the depths of God and the vastness of man and of the created world. But doubt in which only the intellect is used to judge the past model or the past experience is a doubt that will be destructive. Moreover, it will be destructive not only of the model, but of the very possibility of believing in the objective reality which is the object of our contemplation, our communion or our quest. And this is what I feel happened in the period of the Councils. It is what we find in Arius, it is what we find in all the subsequent heretics: an intellectual problem does not correspond to an anaemic, insufficient spiritual experience, and the vigour of the intellect kills the abortive spiritual experience.

What we find in the Church is the contrary. It is the primacy of experience which must be contemplated with all the powers of man, with his intellect, with his heart. I remember two definitions of theology which are entirely alien to what theology is in all its fullness. An introductory phrase in a volume of *Christian Dogmatics* reads, 'Theology is to God what ornithology is to birds'. But this is exactly what it is not. First of all, God is no bird. You cannot catch him in the garden or in the field. You cannot take a film of him. You cannot go around him to see what he looks like from the side and from the tail end. And, what is perhaps even more serious, you cannot do a post-mortem. So you cannot know God and do theology in the way in which you can do ornithology. Another definition of theology I came across some thirty years ago states, 'Theology consists in drawing from scripture all the conclusions one can intellectually draw'. Far from it. Theology is an increasing knowledge of God through communion. It is an act of sharing in God's life, discovering it from within this communion and sharing, and so proclaiming it – nothing less. It involves speaking of God from within the knowledge of God.

We are confronted with such problems in the period of the Councils. But has the Church of the Councils come to an end? I think not. It has not come to an end because the same onslaught of the intellect, the same onslaught of the godless approach to divine things, has continued throughout the ages. It is in action nowadays, within the Church and from without. And if we ask ourselves about heresies and heretics, what their position vis-à-vis the Church is, I would like to point out two things. First, the Church was right in condemning the heresies. But the Church which condemned the heresies from within an experience and a certainty often did so without explaining why this heresy could not be acceptable on the intellectual, rather than the spiritual plane. What I said about Arius, and the fact that in his time the distinction between time and eternity, space and infinity, was not philosophically and scientifically mature, allows people in our days to reason in the same terms. For the Church has not taken advantage of what philosophy and science have discovered and understood about these categories, has not explained what an Athanasius could not explain in his time in scientific or philosophical terms. And that could apply to every other heresy. Thus there is a task for people of our time who are conversant with philosophy or steeped in scientific knowledge. They have to reconsider the ancient heresies and ask themselves whether there is some sort of answer that can now be given from a point of view which is not simply the experiential point of view of the early centuries. For however intellectually mature that was, it failed to solve the problem on the level of the questioner who came from outside.

Secondly, in order to be balanced in our judgement of heresies, we should realise that the Church has been treating heresies in different ways at various epochs. There is a remarkable article published more than half a century ago in *The Christian East* by Metropolitan Antonii Khrapovitskii, one of the narrowest traditional theologians of the Russian Church. Writing on the heresies, and in a manner contrary to what one might expect from him, he notes that the Church took an ever-increasingly lenient attitude to successive heresies throughout the ages (allowing for certain exceptions when an ancient heresy was resurrected under some new guise). And he argues that one can explain this in two different ways. Either one says that the Church's sensitivity to what was true or wrong had diminished, and therefore that the Church, being less and less perceptive, accepted with ever more leniency the successive heresies. This he rejects wholeheartedly, and I think we all can and should reject it. Alternatively, the early heresies rejected elements of the Christian faith that were essential to the very existence of the Christian truth. To deny the divinity of Christ, to deny the humanity of Christ, were two heresies that denied everything involved in Incarnation, and all that it means in terms of the nature of God, of the love of God, of the providence of God, of the nature of man, of the vocation of man, of the destiny of mankind and of the cosmos. Therefore such heresies were to be rejected without any kind of compromise as not being Christianity at all. But Antonii says that as the centuries went by, heresies attached to statements that did not hit at the very heart of the Christian faith. The monothelite discussion,[24] or other more recent heresies of the West or of the East, were such as still accepted essentials which allow those who held them to be considered Christian. And Metropolitan Antonii uses a phrase which I find

---

[24] Monothelite controversy: seventh-century heresy intended to resolve the philosophical difficulties in Christ's divine and human nature, by which it was suggested that he had only one will even if he had two natures. Maximus the Confessor was tortured and exiled for his insistence that Christ had both a human and a divine will. Twenty years after his death his view was accepted by the Sixth Ecumenical Council (680–81).

interesting: in his view every subsequent heresy or group of heretics took away with them an ever-increasing amount of Christian truth and weakened it by the incompleteness of their vision of what was left. Thus subsequent heresies were more Christian and less destructive of the kernel of Christianity. So modern heresies, whichever they are – I would quote the theology of the papacy as one – would still be encompassed by the vision of the undivided Church. And this despite the fact that the teaching introduced something that was profoundly untrue as to the nature of the Church.

The Christian's confrontation with the world

So we must again give thought to what confronts us. In the modern age we are confronted by atheism. We are confronted by non-Christian religions. We are confronted by Christian heresy. We are confronted within the Church by ignorance of our faith and with an anaemic experience of the faith we hold. And all that we must examine most attentively with the same determination, courage and vision as the early

Councils and the early Fathers of the Church faced their own experience. The expression they gave to this experience is something for us to heed: the way in which they could convey this experience in a way understandable to heretics or to outsiders without losing anything of the content or the quality of the message.

We should accordingly also face atheism with more understanding than is often done. For atheism – the loss of God that kills – is rampant outside the Church. It is also rampant within it to the extent to which death has power over us. When Christ identified with mankind, he identified not only with the limitations of a created world, the distortions of the fallen world, the consequences of sin, the needs of mankind in being tired, hungry and thirsty. He accepted to share with us, and not us individually but with mankind in its totality, the loss of God that kills. And when on the Cross he cried, 'My God, my God, why hast thou forsaken me?' (Mark 15:34), he measured in a way in which no atheist ever has or will what it means to be without God and die of it.

So if we look at the surrounding world, the alien world, the pagan world, but particularly at the atheist world, we must realise that even this

world is not outside the sacrificial, tragic, crucified experience of Christ. And we must realise
that our vocation is to understand from within
Christ something which the godless world cannot
understand about itself. This makes us into
another and different Church of the Councils.

We do not hold ecumenical councils, we are
far too disorderly and too divided. But each and
every Christian, each parish, diocese, denomination, is confronted with the same problems as
the undivided Church when it had to face the
outer world, heretical, pagan or godless. And we
also need to go beyond condemnation of it in
order to achieve its salvation.

5

❦❦

'Some of the Faithful Are Perplexed'

*The following is Metropolitan Anthony's response to a letter written by a group of Orthodox Christians at the time when the Russian Orthodox Church began to take part in ecumenical discussions. He presents his view that while the Orthodox Church is the Church of Christ in all her fullness, those outside her who confess in the Spirit that 'Jesus Christ is Lord' are linked with her invisibly, and are only partial strangers to Christ and his salvation. The text was translated by Benedict Roffey from the French original (*Messager de l'Exarchat du Patriarche russe en Europe occidentale, *105–108 (1980–81), pp. 69–77) and published in* Sourozh, *1991, No. 45, pp. 7–16.*

THE LETTER WHICH PROMPTED METROPOLITAN

ANTHONY'S RESPONSE:

Ever since the time when our Patriarchal Church [i.e. the Russian Orthodox Church] began to take part in the ecumenical movement, expressions have begun to appear in our vocabulary which often provoke serious perplexity among the faithful – the more so since these expressions have become so frequently used that we hear them even in the mouth of our own Orthodox bishops, even though their meaning remains obscure.

One very widely used expression which provokes perplexity, if not scandal, is 'the undivided Church' or 'the ancient undivided Church'. When we repeat the Creed, are we not conscious that the Church, the Body of Christ inseparable from its Head, is above all ONE? 'Is Christ divided?' we ask with Saint Paul (1 Cor 1:13).

Not everyone knows the history of the Church, but most of the faithful do know the Epistles of the Apostles and have read in them how some groups of Christians separated themselves from the Church to follow various seducers, or for other reasons. For example, 'all they which are in Asia' turned away from Saint Paul (2 Tim 1:15). And we should also remember those who 'went out from us, but they were not of us' (1 John 2:19), and so on. Throughout the history of the Church, it would seem, there has not been any time when one group or another has not separated itself, either for doctrinal reasons (the heresies), or for 'reasons susceptible of cure' (the schisms), or even to avoid Church discipline (the 'arbitrary assemblies') (cf. the first rule of Saint Basil).

It has sometimes happened that these separated groups were very numerous, or even in a majority in some regions (for example, during the monophysite heresy,[25] or even in Constantinople itself at the time

---

[25] The heresy that in Christ there was only one nature, not two.

of iconoclasm).[26] But whatever may have been the number of those separated and the reasons for their departure, it has never been thought of as causing 'division' in the Church. The Church has always continued to know herself and confess herself above all as the *one* Church. 'Outside the unity of the Body of Christ, who himself cannot be divided,' said Vladimir Lossky, 'the other attributes – holiness, catholicity, apostolicity – can also not exist.'[27] If we think that in our days the Church is 'divided', does that mean that she was divided by each and every defection and has therefore *always* been divided?

In what way, then, is the present situation to be distinguished from earlier situations? Why do we speak of the 'ancient undivided Church', thus obviously implying that in our days she is 'divided'?

We all reject the 'branch theory'.[28] But if we think that the Church is now divided, do we not, by this very fact, subscribe to that theory? It is not particularly important whether the 'branches' be two or twenty in number; what is important is our

---

[26] Eighth- and ninth-century movement to condemn the veneration of icons as idolatry. Declared a heresy by the Second Council of Nicaea, 787. The restoration of the icons is commemorated each year in the Church calendar on the Sunday of Orthodoxy – the first Sunday in Lent.

[27] 'Concerning the third attribute of the Church', in *Messager de l'Exarchat du Patriarche russe en Europe occidentale*, No. 23 [Paris 1950], p. 60.

[28] 'Branch' theory – i.e. that there is one tree and many branches (cf. John 15:5; Rom 11), all of which are equally valid off-shoots of the one true Vine, Christ.

unequivocal confession of a Church which is *one*, just as her Head is one.

REFLECTIONS ON 'SOME OF THE FAITHUL ARE PERPLEXED'

'What God has cleansed, you must not call common' (Acts 10:15)

I have read with deep sympathy – but also with a certain disquiet – the note entitled 'Some of the faithful are perplexed'.

I have read it with a sympathy which doubtless most Orthodox share when they read the bland, irenic declarations of ecumenical committees: self-deluding declarations which affirm that between us and the heterodox there is a unity of Faith which does not exist; declarations which mislead in that they encourage in other Christians the illusion that the unity of which ecumenists dream is already close at hand, whereas such a unity must be founded on an integrity which is without compromise, on a heroic faithfulness to the Truth.

And I have read it with disquiet also, because the 'perplexity' of the signatories seems to me largely founded on a narrow cramped vision of ecclesial reality.

More than forty years ago, nobody was talking of ecumenism and the members of the Patriarchal Church of Paris would not accept anything that was not of impeccable integrity. Christ said, 'I came not to bring peace, but a sword' (Acts 10:34), and this cutting sword, according to Saint Paul, penetrates what is deepest in us, dividing bones from marrow, soul from spirit (Heb 4:12–13). At that time an article appeared which called our attention to the responsibility which weighed upon us and upon our era: the Councils of the early centuries had, this article said, defined definitively and with dazzling clarity our Faith in God, in our Lord, in the Mother of God; they defined the terms of our salvation and the ultimate promises of God; but while they declared the profound nature of the Church, they did not specify its limits. In the nineteenth century Metropolitan Philaret of Moscow was able to say that we know where the Church is, but we cannot say where it is not: 'Our earthly barriers do not mount as high as heaven', he

concluded.[29] And Father Georges Florovsky –
who for many of us was the very voice of Orthodoxy – in a long article on the Church points out
that none of the Christian confessions has defined
in absolute terms the boundaries of the Church.[30]
It is left for our age to reflect profoundly, with
humility, rigour and charity, on the historical
reality which the Christian world presents to us.

No Orthodox would question the fact that the
Church is one, that she is Unity itself: the mystery, the place and the way in which God saves his

---

[29] Metropolitan Philaret of Moscow (1782–1867) was instrumental in restoring to the Russian Church some of its
independence from the State, lost in the 'reforms' of Peter
the Great.

[30] Archpriest Georges Florovsky (1893–1979), a prominent
figure in the first Russian Emigration. In his article, 'The
Limits of the Church' (*Church Quarterly Review*, vol. 117,
1933, pp. 117–31), Florovsky argues that although Cyprian
of Carthage (d. 258) rightly stated that the sacraments of the
Church are accomplished only in the Church, he defined 'in
the Church' too narrowly, since the Tradition of the Church
has never limited its sacramental effectiveness to its canonical boundaries. He concludes that 'the Church continues to
work in the schisms in expectation of that mysterious hour
when the stubborn heart will be melted in the warmth of
God's pre-eminent grace. When the will and thirst for
commonality and unity will finally burst into flame. The
"validity" of the sacraments among schismatics is the mysterious guarantee of their return to catholic plentitude and
unity.'

creatures and unites himself to them. She is the
Body of Christ, the temple of the Holy Spirit, the
kingdom already 'come with power' (Mark 9:1),
the miracle which makes of us children of God –
and she gives us the possibility of becoming
'partakers of the divine nature' (2 Pet 1:4).

No Orthodox believer doubts the fact that it
is the Orthodox Church, in a unique way and
without equal, which is this mystery, this place,
this kingdom.

Yet in spite of this there remains a problem –
at once theological and moral: what place do we
assign to those who, by choice or because they
were born without any possibility of knowing
Orthodoxy, do not belong to her?

The simplest solution is to exclude them from
the mystery of the Church; to consider it
impossible for them to be attached to the
Church: to declare that one either belongs to the
Church, or does not, to say that since the Church
is Unity itself, any breach implies exclusion, a
cutting-off which is either self-willed or surgically
applied. That was the theological position of our
own Metropolitan Elevferii,[31] for whom any

---

[31] Metropolitan Elevferii (Bogoiavlenskii), representative
abroad of Metropolitan Sergius (head of the Russian
Orthodox Church in the Stalinist era).

departure from the Orthodox faith implied a total estrangement from the Church with the most radical consequences: neither divine grace, nor sacraments nor priesthood could exist, and this applied not only amongst the heretics, but also even in schismatic communities. Is such a conception tenable? The history of the Church and her theology seems to me incompatible with this attitude – simple and convenient though it may be – for it denies the existence of any of the serious problems which have to be faced by a position that is worthy of God.

The very notions of heresy and schism imply a relationship to the Faith of the Church and a lasting relationship – however painful this may be – between the Church and those who have separated themselves from her. We do not accuse the Muslims or the Buddhists either of heresy or of schism; they are simply strangers for us. To be heretical or schismatic, one has to be Christian!

Some may reply, perhaps, that those who are in error can, in a sense, be considered Christians, but they are not members of the Church. But is this really possible? Can one be a Christian *outside* the Church? Can one proclaim 'Jesus Christ is Lord' (Phil 2:11) otherwise than by the Holy Spirit? (And is not this the teaching of Saint John as well as Saint Paul?) Is it thinkable or even in practice possible, to be instructed by the Spirit, to become the place of his presence, and to remain a stranger to the Church? Does not the conversion of Cornelius in the Book of the Acts[32] assure us of the contrary? Can one live under the inspiration of the Holy Spirit and yet remain a stranger to Christ? Or be 'in Christ' and yet 'outside the Church'? When 'outside the Church there is no salvation'?

And what are we to say, what are we to do with those who have embraced a false faith, accepted a defective theology, yet live and die for Christ? Must not his witnesses, martyrs for their faith in our Lord – Catholics, Protestants and others – who have lived only to make their Saviour known to those who did not know him, who have lived heroic lives, who have accepted a painful death, be known by Christ in eternity? And *can* they then be rejected by his disciples on earth? Do we not read in the Gospel that, having returned from one of their missions, the Apostles reported to the Lord that they had met a man who was performing miracles in the name of Jesus Christ and that they had forbidden him to

---

[32] Cf. Acts 10.

do so. 'Do not stop him,' the Lord replied. 'No one who has accomplished a miracle in my name can afterwards blaspheme against me' (Mark 9:39).

What is heresy?

What does the history of the Church teach us about heresies? In an article which is already quite old, preceding by about twenty years the birth of the ecumenical movement, Metropolitan Anthony (Khrapovitsky)[33] who, without offence to his memory, one may call an *integrist*, asks why the behaviour of the Church with regard to heresies has changed over the centuries, moving from 'strictness' to 'economy'. The simplest and most cynical reply would be to recognise sadly and with a feeling of shame, that the conscience of the faithful having become weak where dogma is concerned, they were no longer able to discern with clarity the true from the false, they ceased to be offended and more and more easily accepted error, relativising it more and more, in proportion

---

[33] Metropolitan Anthony (Khrapovitsky) (1863–1936), the first Chief Hierarch of the Russian Orthodox Church Outside Russia (ROCOR).

to the extent to which their own sense of God and of the Truth was dimmed. To accept such a vision of things would be to deny the presence and the constant action of the Spirit of God in the Church. It would be to deny the Church.

Another explanation seems to Metropolitan Anthony more true – and seems to me to express both the historical wisdom of Orthodoxy and the dogmatic wisdom of the Church. The latter has never concentrated her attention in an exclusive manner on evil, on error. While recognising with horror error and evil, she has always been attentive to what remained of inspired Truth in the teaching or the practice of those who detached themselves from her: 'The light shines in the darkness, and the darkness has not overcome it' (John 1:5). It is not only for the purity of her doctrine or of her Christian life that the Church is concerned, but for the salvation of her lost children. Did not a spiritual writer say that the most sinister heretic, at the moment when he reads the Gospel to his flock of lost sheep, proclaims the Word of God and is 'in the Truth'?

Orthodoxy was severe without compromise with regard to the earliest heresies because they rejected what is essential to the Faith, the divinity of Christ and his humanity, thereby denying the witness of God and the mystery of our salvation. But subsequent heresies, in spite of their errors, retained an increasingly rich Christian content which was less and less incomplete, more and more able to assure the salvation of these dogmatically and spiritually impoverished communities. And the Church, discerning the presence of the good grain amidst the tares, has treated these dissident communities with growing comprehension. It is impossible to place at the same level the errors of the Roman Catholics or of the Protestants and those of the Gnostics, the Arians or the Manicheans.

We have in the religious literature of the first centuries and in the lives of the saints witnesses which, although questionable from a strictly historical point of view, nevertheless show us the attitude of the Church. Here are a few, taken from *The Spiritual Meadow* of John Moschos.[34]

A Christian who, in ignorance, has got himself baptised by an heretical priest, asks for baptism by an Orthodox bishop. The latter, however,

---

[34] *The Spiritual Meadow* (*Pratum Spirituale*) by John Moschos, a monk of the Judaean desert in the late sixth century. Travelling frequently between the monastic centres of Egypt, Syria, Palestine and Asia Minor, Moschos collected and compiled stories of monastic life.

fearing to repeat a valid baptism, gets the heretical priest to be present so as to make sure that it really was he who had baptised the candidate. On seeing the heretic the candidate cried out: 'O no! He did not baptise me. It was a luminous being. As for him, I did indeed see him: two demons were holding him in chains in the corner of the church while I was being baptised ...'

Again, a saintly priest, but not very well informed, belongs to one of the heresies of his time. His deacon held on to the true Faith, however, and is troubled to see such a pious man, such a pure man, living in error. After much hesitation he points it out to him. 'It is not possible!' the priest cries. 'Whenever I celebrate, two angels of light assist me. Would they agree to concelebrate with a heretic? I shall put the question to them!' And next day, after the consecration of the Holy Gifts, the priest suspends the celebration and asks them whether really he is in error. 'Yes,' reply the angels. 'But,' cries the priest, 'why did you not tell me? How can you have left me in heresy?' 'The Lord commanded us to wait until the deacon bore witness to his love of God and of you by telling you himself. If he had not done so, we would have spoken.' 'But how could you celebrate with me?' the poor man cried. 'God,' replied the angels, 'receives your prayers and your offerings because of the purity of your heart.'

Saint Augustine, too, was able to write, 'Many are they who on earth believed themselves strangers to the Church but on the Day of Judgment will find that they belonged to her; many also, alas, are they who will have thought themselves to be members of the Church and who will discover that they are strangers to her.'

So to be a heretic, one must be – or want to be – a Christian! Otherwise, one can only be either a pagan or an apostate. It is not those who have said, 'Lord, Lord!', nor even those who have 'eaten in the house of the Lord' whom Christ will recognise as his own, but those who have done the will of God (cf. Matt 7).

A light shining in the darkness

So what is Orthodoxy and where are we to place this paradox of the Church? How are we to resolve this tension between the Absolute, which can accept no compromise, and the becoming, the slow conquest of a lost world by God the Saviour?

In one of our conversations, Father Soph-rony[35] said to me one day: 'Nobody has the right to say that he is Orthodox in the strict and absolute meaning of the word, for to be Ortho-dox is to know God as he is and to serve and adore him in the full measure of his holiness.' In this sense, we are at one and the same time *in patria* and *in via* – in port and on the way. All has been accomplished by God and in Christ, but all has not been brought to fruition, either in us or in the world. The Church is not the assembly of saints; she is the throng of repentant sinners – and 'repentant' here means 'turned towards God', like Peter drowning in the storm. Is it not legitimate to say that where there is a knowledge of God, recognition of Christ by the Holy Spirit, the gift of one's life and of one's death to the Lord, then Orthodoxy is present, and so also the Church, as light purified and flashing forth, as life-bearing water penetrating the parched earth, as leaven raising the dough, as the blood finding a passage for itself through damaged tissue?

How painful it is to see the light obscured, but

---

[35] Archimandrite Sophrony (Sakharov) (1896–1993), disciple and biographer of St Silouan of Mount Athos, and founder of the Monastery of St John the Baptist, Tolleshunt Knights, Essex.

how wonderful to see that the shadows can neither extinguish it nor even completely hide it!
Is not the Triumph of Orthodoxy,[36] which we
celebrate at the beginning of Lent, precisely this
triumph of God over us (and not that of the
Orthodox over their adversaries), and ought we
not to be glad at the thought of a presence,
imperceptible to our eyes but visible for God, his
angels and his saints, of a germ of life amidst
seeds of death, of healthy tissues surviving
amidst tissues that are attacked by gangrene, or
cancer? Should not these seeds of salvation be
dear to us, rather than letting ourselves feel
repulsion or revolt at the signs of grave illness, of
a disorder which can kill those for whom Christ
has lived and given his life? Archbishop Alexis of
Dusseldorf used to say that the Truth, Life and
the Church are like a candle burning in the midst
of the universe. It seems to warm and light up
only a little space, and yet as far as the infinity of
space extends, darkness is no longer absolute.
Since the time Christ achieved his victory, his
Spirit is in the world – active, life-giving, taking
the initiative in our salvation, fashioning in the
heart of all who search for the Absolute, however

---

[36] Cf. note 26.

they may name it, the image of the living God, watching over the embers which have survived the great winds of heresy and schism, stirring them, making them glow once more.

Perhaps this is the right moment to recall an image which was dear to Lev Zander[37] and was presented by him in a courageous book called *Vision and Action*, a book full of wisdom and hope, of faith and of understanding, but which was criticised very unfairly. He distinguishes – I would prefer to say 'discerns', in the sense in which Saint Paul speaks of discerning spirits – three stages in the process of separation: divergence, immobility and convergence. At the moment when two convictions clash, their adherents can only turn from one another; without yet having separated, and while they are still back-to-back, they have turned towards different horizons and can only deny each other. So close still, they are yet already infinitely far apart. Their glances no longer meet; they can no longer reveal their souls by looking one another in the eye.

---

[37] Fr Lev Zander (1893–1964), first general secretary of the Russian Student Christian Movement in exile, ecumenist and author of the book *Vision and Action* (London, 1952), on the ecumenical movement.

Years of silence then pass and personal resentment dies down. There remain only the real subjects of their dispute – and hanging over them, the desire of the two antagonists to be faithful to God and to his Truth. Now the adversaries can turn round the one towards the other and ask themselves what has become of the erstwhile friend who had become the symbol of error. What remains in him of his original beauty? They will ask at first with curiosity, then with anxiety, whether the demon has vanquished those who believed themselves to be faithful to God, however grave their errors. Distant forms emerge from the mist, confused sounds, a language which is no longer understood makes itself heard ... then – and is this simple curiosity or a more noble concern for the destiny of the 'other'? – after a period of stalemate which pushes and pulls the groups towards one another, come the questions. Who are you? What has become of you throughout the centuries of separation? What have you learnt? What have you understood? How do I seem to you? Are you the Prodigal Son at his departure or at his return? Or are you still in a far country? Are you living in artificial wealth and glory, surrounded by false friends? Or are you alone, poor, hungry, humiliated? Do you still remember the Father's house? Can you still pronounce the holy word, 'Father'? Have you reached that degree of despair which will enable you to recognise your faults, your errors, to take the step without which you cannot become again what you have always been for your Father, the Son, the Lost Sheep; to recognise also the Cross of suffering?

Is it not in this way that the Christian confessions are rediscovering one another in these days? Certainly we are a long way from that unity of which so much is said! Doctrinal sensitivity has been watered down in the heterodox world, while attachment remains strong to conceptions which are incompatible with the Gospel message (papal primacy and infallibility; the *filioque*; spiritual and doctrinal anti-palamism; the theory of 'branches' in the Church; predestination; in its extreme form, salvation by faith alone). But some non-Orthodox communities are beginning to recognise themselves within Orthodoxy. Is this surprising? Are we not *their own past*, we might say, while they are neither our present nor our future?

The true measure of Orthodoxy

It is our task to fill our gaze on the seeds of Life, on what there is of the authentic Truth in their communions, and not to confuse heresy, schism and apostasy. We must remind ourselves of two things which are easily forgotten: first, that the ancient – and the modern – heresies have justly been condemned, but also that too often no reply has been given to the problems – philosophical, theological or moral – from which they had their birth, for no error is born of simple ill will; and, in the second place, we must not forget that often we are separated from one another by the language which we use, and also that often similar terms, even identical terms, cover meanings which are sufficiently different to be incompatible – the letter triumphing over the spirit.

But we must also never forget that it is easy and natural for us to consider the whole of our Faith and of our practice as the true measure of Orthodoxy, whereas very many of the things which are dear to us are only the temporary, human, even accidental reflection of absolute realities.

It was enough for the eunuch to recognise

Christ as his Saviour for him to be baptised.[38] Do
we not ask more of those who want to return to
the Faith of their fathers than we do of our own
people, born in our own Faith? How numerous
are the Orthodox-in-name who live by super-
stitions which are incompatible with a healthy
faith, who float between ignorance and heresy,
who only appear in church for baptism, marriage
or burial, and who have the right to lay claim on
their 'Orthodoxy' so as to receive the sacraments
of the Church, which we refuse – with good
reason, and which we are obliged to refuse – to
those who come from another Christian community? And do we not betray Christ by our way
of life?[39] Do we not publicly deny his message
when we trample underfoot his commandments?
Is not that a heresy in act and deed?[40] The
Church is One. And it is the Orthodox Church
which, on earth, is that Church: holy with the
holiness of God in his theandric nature, in his
mystery, but carrying that which is holy in a
vessel of clay; knowing God in the silence of

---

[38] Cf. Acts 8.

[39] Cf. Rom 2:24: 'The name of God is blasphemed among the
gentiles because of you.'

[40] Cf. 1 John 2:9: 'He who says he is in the light and hates his
brother is in the darkness still.'

contemplation; stammering out his witness from century to century in terms which, however exact they may be in terms of human language, can never give a full account of God and of his ways.

Does not Saint Paul, speaking of the Church of his time, say that disagreements are inevitable in the Church, but that they are there so that those who possess a greater wisdom may be recognised.[41] The Church is indestructible, the gates of hell will not prevail against her; but her way forward is far from being simple. The Truth, possessed in the depths of contemplative souls, can only be expressed through a long and painful struggle between silence and speech, between the Infinite, the Eternal and the finite, the ephemeral. It is a knowledge of God which is in the process of emerging into the light, and it cannot avoid passing through trials and errors. It is indeed the Wisdom of God that those who have the greater wisdom must manifest to the world, and it is in obedience and humility that human reason must give way to divine Reason. And it is there that asceticism intervenes, the renunciation of self.

In a strict sense, even the Church of the Apostles and martyrs had its crises, tensions and

---

[41] 1 Cor 11:19.

divisions. Nevertheless, the Church remained One and God triumphed. When people speak of the 'undivided Church' it is of this period that we think, it is of her that we dream; of the time when, instead of confrontation, there was a sharing of problems, of hesitations over the formulation of the Truth as a tenable intellectual thesis, when there was a great and humble pastoral patience which knew how *not* to hurry, which was attentive enough *not* to strangle a seed of life, whose whole concern was the salvation of the sinner, the return of the Prodigal. Saint Paul could say that it was on milk that he had at first nourished his spiritual children; that he had made himself all things to all men in the hope of saving at least some of those for whom Christ died on the Cross. And he could do it because he had faith in all men of good will (Rom 2:14) and because he was ready to die for the salvation of his people, the people of God (Rom 9:3).

No! The Church is not divided! She is One now as in the past. And we see her plenitude in Orthodoxy through the faith which renders transparent the human destiny of the fallen world which is in the process of 'becoming'. But her mystery goes beyond her visible limits. It is impossible to speak of 'the Church' on the one hand and of 'the Christian World' on the other, so as to spare the non-Orthodox some illusions, from which they awaken with bitterness when they know us better. But we ourselves, we must never forget nor cease to see the mysterious ways of God in the souls and communities separated from the Church, from her who is and remains for ever – in spite of the scandal of a Church full of tensions – not an isolated column, but rather a Pillar called upon to carry the weight of the world, the Pillar of Truth.

PART III

❦ ❦

The True Nature of
Hierarchy

6

✿ ✿

The Hierarchical Structures of the Church

Under Metropolitan Anthony, and then Bishop Basil, the Diocesan Assembly of Sourozh met twice yearly at the Russian Orthodox Cathedral at Ennismore Gardens in London, and its meetings always included a 'major topic of discussion' so that members should have something of value to think about as well as dealing with administrative items. On 12 June 1993, Metropolitan Anthony introduced the discussion with the following talk, which was also published in Sourozh, *1993, No. 53, pp. 1–8.*

Our calling as members of the Church

When we speak of the Church we can speak of it from two angles. The catechism tells us that the Church is a body of people who are united by the same hierarchy, the same doctrine, the same liturgy, etc. But this is a very external way of approaching things, very much like describing to someone what a church building looks like.

But the Church is known from within. And the inside of the Church is something that cannot be defined in any of these terms, singly or taken together, because the Church is a living organism, a body. In the nineteenth century Samarin[42] defined the Church as an 'organism of love'. It is a body which is both human and divine. It is a body of people who are connected with God not only by faith or by hope or by longing or by promise, but much more organically. It is the place where God and his creation have already met and are at one. It is the very mystery of this meeting. It is the way in which one can enter into this relationship.

The Church is human in two different ways: in us – who are in the making, as it were – and in Christ, who is the revelation of what we are called to be, every one of us singly. On the other hand, the Church is also the temple of the Holy Spirit. But we – individually, singly – are also called to be the dwelling-place of the Spirit. And so both the Church at large – all those who are

---

[42] Yuri A. Samarin (1819–79), a member of the Slavophile movement, who wrote the preface to the first edition of Khomiakov's theological works.

members of the Church – and each one of those members, is possessed of the Holy Spirit, possessed in the sense that we cannot possess the Holy Spirit, but he gives himself to us and we are pervaded by his presence, to a greater or lesser extent according to our openness to him and our faithfulness to Christ – our faithfulness to what we are called to be, to the perfect image of the perfect, total, real man. And in Christ and in the Spirit we are the children of God.

We think of ourselves very often as of adopted children. Christ is the only-begotten Son and we are, as it were, his brothers and sisters. This is the way he speaks of us – as his friends.[43] But we are on this level only because we have not reached the full stature of Christ. We are called to grow into a likeness of Christ that will allow us to see in each of us – and in all of us collectively – what St Irenaeus tells us is our vocation: that in Christ and by the power of the Holy Spirit we are called to become not only adopted children of God but the only Son of God, as a whole body. And the fact that we can be told that we are called to be the only Son of God, all of us together, shows

---

[43] Cf. Jn 15:15.

how total our oneness should be, how complete our oneness should be.

An icon of the Trinity

This is something important. And when we speak of structures we must remember that this is the essence, the reality of the Church, and all other things just serve this purpose. We are on our way to this fullness. But the Church *is* already, incipiently, this fullness. We are already children of the Kingdom. The Kingdom has already come into the world. We are all its citizens. And yet we are citizens that must, each of us, grow to the full stature of Christ; that is, we must acquire what Paul calls 'the mind of Christ' (1 Cor 2:16). We must become so filled with the Spirit that our every word, every thought, every movement of our inner self – and indeed, even of our bodies – should be filled with the Spirit. As Father Silouan of Mount Athos[44] said, the grace of God that reaches us in the spirit gradually pervades our soul and fills in the end our body, so that body, soul and spirit become a single

---

[44] Silouan of Mount Athos (1866–1938): well-loved Russian saint, ascetic, and monk of Mount Athos.

spiritual reality at one with Christ, so that we become – not only incipiently, progressively – real members, real limbs of one Body.

When we think of the relationships between the constitutive parts of this body, of these limbs – St Paul speaks of the eye and the head and the foot and so on – we must realise that our vocation, and the vocation of the Church, is to be an icon of the Holy Trinity. The only real structure, the only real way in which the Church can be formed so as to fulfil its vocation is by expressing in all its being all these relationships within the Holy Trinity: relationships of love, relationships of freedom, relationships of holiness, and so forth.

In the Holy Trinity we find what the Greek writers call the 'monarchy' of the Father. He is the source, the heart of the divinity. But the Spirit and the Son are equal to him; they are not by-products, they are not secondary gods, they are what he is. And we are to ask ourselves: what then? How can we be on earth an icon of this reality?

May I suggest, but only suggest, that for us the apex, the extreme point in this situation is the Lord Jesus Christ. The Lord Jesus Christ is our Lord, our God, our Saviour, and it is from him that all the structure begins – a structure which is pervaded by the presence of the Holy Spirit and which, in the Spirit and in Christ, makes us gradually, imperfectly to begin with, an image of the Holy Trinity. And when I say an image I do not mean simply a static structure but something as dynamically powerful, as dynamically alive as the Holy Trinity itself.

Some of the Fathers of the Church have spoken of the life of the Holy Trinity as *perichoresis*, a round, a dance, in which the three persons occupy in the simultaneity of timelessness one another's position. They are to one another what the other is to them, all the time, at every moment. And this is what we are called to be.

If this is the case, then there are two elements in the life of the Church. The one element which by necessity is structured because we are imperfect, because we are on our way, because we must be guided and, like a river that runs towards the sea, must have banks, since otherwise we will become a bog. And on the other hand, there is the living water which Christ gave to the Samaritan woman that runs in this river.

There is in us already something which is fulfilled and something which is imperfect. To continue this image of an icon, not only each of us singly but the Church as a whole is very much like an icon that was painted perfect but has been damaged by human carelessness, by circumstances, by hatred, by all the evils of the world, so that what is noticeable to the outer eye, to the eye of a person alien to the Church, is that some parts of it are still perfect beauty while the rest is a mess of destruction. And our own personal vocation, in our own life and in the community to which we belong – and this may be the parish, the eucharistic community, the diocese, the wider local Church or the Church universal – is to restore this icon to its perfect beauty, a beauty which is already there.

St Ephraim of Syria said that when God creates a human being he puts at the core of his or her being the fullness of the Kingdom of God. If you prefer, one can say that he puts there the perfect image of God. And the purpose of life is to dig, deeper and deeper, until we reach this point and bring it to the fore. So when we speak of structures in the Church, we must remember that there is in the Church something which cannot be structured, cannot be organised, cannot be limited by rules and by laws. This is the action of the Holy Spirit within each of us, and within the local body, or the body universal. And this is very important because the Holy Spirit speaks to us, each of us and all of us, either in inexpressible groanings or with the clarity of the trumpet that calls us into battle.

But on the other hand, there is in us imperfection and frailty. And therefore there must be structures that are like a scaffolding, or like the banks of a river, or like a stick which one uses if one is lame, to prevent us from collapsing.

Now the temptation for the Church, as for every other human organisation, is to structure itself according to worldly principles, principles of hierarchy, of power – as a hierarchy of submission, a hierarchy of enslavement, of humiliation, of irrelevance. Take the hierarchy of irrelevance, for instance. In more than one community – practically speaking, very much in our Orthodox communities, and theologically in Rome – the laity is an irrelevance. It is a flock to be guided. It has no right in and of itself except to obey, to be directed towards the goal which, allegedly, the hierarchy knows.

In its extreme form, the Church is conceived as a pyramid at the top of which stands the Pope. To me, this is a heresy against the nature of the Church, because no one but the Lord Jesus Christ has a right to stand at the top of that pyramid. It is not a question of whether this means that the Church will be well administered, but of the very nature of the Church.

So if we eliminate the structures of power and the submission that goes with them, we must still ask ourselves what should be the structure of the Church. The structure which we are entitled to speak of is that which Christ defines when he says, 'If anyone wants to be first, let him be a servant to all' (Mark 9:35). The hierarchy consists in service. The higher the servant allegedly is in rank, in titles, the lower he should be in terms of service. He should be the one who does the humblest service, and not the highest.

I was once asked by a journalist in France why is it that we Christians are so arrogant as to have titles like 'Your Eminence' – this was addressed to me personally – and I said, 'Why not? It is a sign of our ultimate humility. There are mountains, there are hills, and there are mole hills' – which in French is called *une eminence*, a little hill. From a theological point of view I think this was a true answer. That is exactly what the patriarch, the metropolitan, the archbishop, the bishop, the clergy and so forth should be: part of a pyramid directed upwards, they being at the root, the pyramid standing on one point, which is the greatest hierarch, the lowest servant. This is something which we must recapture.

But it can be recaptured only if we recapture our understanding of the Church as a total body with a variety of functions and not a variety of bodies joined together one on top of the other. By this I mean that we must recapture the role, the dignity of the laity. We have just had a diocesan conference on the royal priesthood.[45] The royal priesthood is forgotten. If it is not forgotten in manuals of theology, it is forgotten in the practice of life. And I would like to insist on that because I would like you to accept a point of view which is very important to me: dear to me and important to me.

By becoming a minister of the Church we do not stop being a member of the Body of Christ, of the *laos*, of the people of God. I was once introduced to a conference from which clergy were banned, but where I had to be admitted because I was a speaker, with the words: 'Here is Metropolitan Anthony, who is a layman in clerical orders'.

This is perfectly true. The laity, on one level, includes also the clergy, but with different

---

[45] Conference of the Diocese of Sourozh at Effingham, Kent.

functions. We must recapture this notion of the holiness and dignity of the laity. And unless we do this, we cannot think of structures that are an image of the Holy Trinity. We do not have in the Holy Trinity – I am about to say something quite blasphemous – a 'top dog' with subservient slaves. God the Father is not the 'boss' of the Trinity, with two 'managers'. It is true that the Fathers say that God creates the world with his two hands, the Son and the Holy Spirit. This is imagery applicable in that context. But basically there is a total equality of the three Persons of the Trinity. And there is also a total equality of all the members of the Church. There is no other way.

Of course, there is a hierarchical structure: a structure in which the one who is the best servant, who is the slave of others, is greatest in the eyes of God. But that is the point. This is made even less visible thanks to our liturgical practice, because our eucharistic Liturgy has in its forms very much taken as a model the Byzantine Imperial Court. And so it is not difficult for a bishop to feel himself as the head of the body, surrounded by lesser and lesser ministers, and then a flock outside. But this is untrue.

The Liturgy is celebrated by the whole body,

not by the ministers alone. And this is why I have said more than once that no one should come and receive communion who has not been present from the beginning of the service – unless, of course, a major impediment intervenes. Because otherwise he is not *making* the Liturgy. If someone arrives halfway through the Liturgy and claims to have communion, he is treating the Liturgy as though it were a restaurant in which various cooks are preparing the meal: he comes when he has the time and claims his portion.

This is very important: we must recover the notion that the laity *includes* the clergy. And in that case the different members of the ordained ministry will have their own proper place in the building of the Church.

Our vocation as human beings

The vocation of man, from the beginning, from the first chapter of Genesis, has been to sanctify the whole creation of God. St Gregory Palamas[46] tells us that man was created belonging to two

---

[46] Gregory Palamas (1296–1359): monk of Mount Athos and later Archbishop of Thessalonika; champion of the hesychast movement.

worlds: the world of God (the spiritual world) and the world of matter. And not – this is my parenthesis – not because he is the summit of a process of evolution, the most perfect monkey becoming an imperfect man and then developing into something else. Man was not created out of the most perfect monkey. He was, according to the Bible, created of the dust of the earth. God took what is the basic material of creation and made man out of it, so that man participates in everything that was created out of dust, beginning with the smallest atom and ending with the greatest galaxy, and all the rest of the visible created world around us, plants, animals, etc.

This has an enormous importance. If God became man in Christ, then Christ participates, as does each of us, in the dust, in the galaxies, in the atom, in the animal world, in everything which belongs to the created world. He has taken upon himself the experience of all createdness. He is one of us, but in him everything created can see itself, having reached the final term of its vocation and growth.

Again, when we think of the bread and wine in the Liturgy, the bread and wine remain bread and wine in the sense that they do not become something other than they are. And yet by being filled by the power of the Holy Spirit they become the Body and Blood of Christ – without ceasing to be what they are. In the same way we are called to become the sons of God without ceasing to be the unique person each of us is. Each of us is unique before God, and not just one of many similar samples of humanity. The Book of Revelation says to us that at the end of time everyone will receive a name which only he and God know, a name which is the total expression of what he is in essence, in his unique relationship with God.[47]

A hierarchy of humility

And so when we speak of hierarchy we need to realise that we must recapture a true approach to hierarchy: a hierarchy of service, a hierarchy of humility, a hierarchy in which there is no dominion, no power. God chose to be powerless when he gave us freedom, the right to say 'no' to whatever he says. But God in Christ, God in the Spirit has another quality. Not power, which is the ability to coerce, but authority, which is the

[47] Cf. Rev. 2:17.

ability to convince. And that is a very different thing.

Authority is that quality which a human being – and God – possesses of being able to convince, not force us to do something. And if our hierarchy learns, gradually, that the vocation of the hierarchy is to have authority and not power, we will come nearer to becoming what the Church is called to be: a living body, an 'organism of love' – but not of sentimentality. For love is described by Christ when he says no one has greater love than he or she who gives his or her life for his or her neighbour.

And so when we speak of the structures of the Church – yes, they are a necessity. But the attitude of the people who are 'in command' must be that of the servant. 'I am in your midst as the one who serves,' says Christ. And we are called to be servants as *he* is a servant. There are structures that are of necessity because of our frailty, because of our sinfulness, because of the temptations which the devil puts before us, because of our immaturity. But all of these should be like the Law of the Old Testament, which St Paul calls a *paidagogos*, one who teaches, who guides.

And when we read in the beginning of Genesis that man was given dominion, we interpret it always in terms of the right to govern, to enslave, to subdue and to tread all creatures underfoot. In reality the word 'dominion' in English and French comes from the Latin word *dominus,* which may mean 'overlord', but can mean 'teacher', 'guide' or 'master'. Our role is to be masters guiding the whole of creation into the fullness of unity with God, not to dominate. But in this process, as I said, structures are necessary. There is need for a formal ministry.

Sacramental ministry

Why a ministry at all? May I suggest – and this is my surmise, so anyone more theologically qualified than I am should put me in my place – that every human being is called to bring into the realm of God everything that surrounds him: the circumstances of life, the places, the beings. But there is one thing which cannot be done by man: he cannot sanctify himself beyond himself. We cannot by an act of will, by our own choice, become what we are not, because we have fallen away from our vocation. And this is the point at which Christ and the Holy Spirit enter into the world, become active, and commit to us two things: a sacramental ministry, that is, priests whose vocation is to bring forth to God the elements of this created world so that they can be taken out of the context of sin and brought into the context of God; and then God takes them on and sanctifies them by the strength of the Holy Spirit.

This is the essence of ministry. The administrative aspect of it is something incidental; it is not the essence. And so we find ourselves with a structured laity, a *laos*, to which the clergy belong, a clergy whose vocation is to celebrate, to perform actions – or rather to create situations in which God can act; because if you think of the Liturgy, the Liturgy *can* be celebrated and *is* celebrated by no one but Christ himself. He is the only High Priest of all creation. We can say words, we can make gestures, but the one who brings forth these gifts to God is Christ, and the power that transmutes these gifts into the Body of Christ and the Blood of Christ, that transforms the waters which we bring from the well into the waters of life eternal, is the Holy Spirit.

7

Primacy and Primacies in the Church

The problems posed by 'primacy' in the Church have been with us from the beginning: the earliest attempt at a solution can be seen in the 'Apostolic Council' described in Acts 15 and the question still remains the central area of disagreement between the Orthodox and the Roman Catholic Church. On 29 November 1982 Metropolitan Anthony devoted his 'Constantinople Lecture' to this subject, in a series established to commemorate the Second Ecumenical Council of AD 381. In it he speaks critically of the notion of primacy as it has developed in both East and West. The lecture was transcribed, and published in Sourozh, *1986, No. 25, pp. 6–15.*

Canon 3 of the First Council of Constantinople deals with this very subject that I have chosen to speak about. It defines the position of two sees in Christendom, that of Rome and that of Constantinople, and declares that Rome is to occupy the first place in rank of honour because it is the city of the Emperor, while Constantinople is to occupy the second place because it is the second capital of the Empire. This definition is of great importance, because it underlines very clearly that there was no theological basis for establishing such an order of precedence. It was only expediency – both political and practical – that defined their positions.

But it is not specifically about this canon that I want to speak. I want to attract your attention to the wider problem of 'primacy and primacies' in the Church at large. In the mid-1930s Vladimir Lossky, in his first lecture on the history of the Church, indicated that there are three themes that run through the whole of the Church's history: groping for and proclaiming the truth; structuring the Church so that it corresponds as closely as possible to its nature; and thirdly, the directives given on the spiritual life of the Church. These three elements are essential if we want to understand what the Church is and how it should be built, structured, and find its expression in history.

We have, however, several problems that confront us. First of all, in the course of the early centuries, the Church defined the essentials of the Christian faith: the doctrine of the Holy Trinity, the relationship between Father, Son and Holy Spirit, and so on. But we still have no conciliar definition of the Church as such, one which can be used by all Christians. In the course of centuries the Church was aware of its nature, of its life, of its dynamic. It proclaimed the Gospel and lived by it, and yet the Church remains to a very great extent mysterious, not just when we try to speak of its deepest nature, but also when we try to define its limits and indicate where it is and where it is not. There is no one denomination in Christendom that has, in the course of the whole of the Church's history of its practically 2000 years, given such a definition of the Church that would allow us not only to define what the Church is in essence, but also its limits. Perhaps this is not accidental, for it may well be that we must live a long time before we can perceive and understand sufficiently the nature of the Church to combine in such a definition a theological vision that reflects both the Church in God, in its essence, and its historical situation.

We are to a very great extent, as far as the Church is concerned, prisoners of history. In many ways we are also prisoners of certain theological presuppositions that have gradually been accepted without sufficient consideration.

We are prisoners of history in that somehow what *has* happened seems gradually to have become what *should* happen. We have this canon of Constantinople concerning 'primacy and primacies' which arose in a historical situation which itself was rooted in a political situation and in practical expediency. And yet gradually, because in the course of centuries we have become accustomed to the status quo, it has become, in the eyes of many, a mark of the Church. It seems to many that this is how things should be.

Yet the situation has changed, history has moved on, and the relative importance of these cities has become infinitely different from what it was. Nevertheless, the formulation stands, and illusions are very often based on it. One could even say that this use of history has forced upon the Church a view which was not born of theology but of accident: the Roman Catholic view of the papacy. The primacy of Peter – not so much of Peter, but of the successors of Peter – has resulted in a gradual evolution which we Orthodox consider to be both unfortunate and destructive for the Church. The Pope becomes not only a sign of unity, but also a ruler seen at certain moments in a light which would probably make many a Roman Catholic shudder today. In a very interesting book by a Roman Catholic historian and theologian, for five years a member of the Vatican Secretariat for Christian Unity, there are quotations showing how, having begun with considerations of expediency, one particular local church reached the most incredible conclusions.[48]

In the times of Pius IX it was stated very clearly that the Pope was God's representative on earth, writes August Hasler. One enthusiast called the Pope 'vice-God of humanity'. An official journal of the Vatican says, in the words of one of the bishops, that 'when the Pope meditates, it is God who thinks in him'. Bishop Berteaud of Tulle in France describes the Pope as 'the word of God made flesh, living in our midst'. The suffragan bishop of Geneva, Gaspare Mermillod, 'did not hesitate', says the author, 'to speak of a threefold incarnation of the Son of God: in the Virgin's womb, in the Eucharist, and in the old man of the Vatican'.

I know that today such expressions would be rejected, that most Roman Catholics would never accept such a position. But it is quite clear

---

[48] August Bernhard Hasler, *How the Pope Became Infallible* (1979).

that these expressions were gradually born of a basic attitude that falsified a root relationship between the Church and its bishops, between the Church and the primatial sees that have gradually emerged from history, but not from the Gospel.

Here we find ourselves at a point of tension which belongs to the very nature of the Church. The Church is an eschatological body, a mysterious body – I shall say a few words about this in a moment – and at the same time a body which evolves, acts, grows and goes through tragedy and glory in history.

The mystery of the Church consists in the fact that it is a body, a living organism which is simultaneously and equally both human and divine. The 'firstborn from the dead', our Lord Jesus Christ, crucified and risen, is the living God, the Son of God become the Son of Man. And in him – through him – God is present in the Church from the first moment of the Incarnation. The Church is no longer separable from the divine, because Christ is God.

Then, after his Resurrection, on two different occasions and in two different manners, the first described in John 20 and the second in the Book of Acts, Christ gave to his Church the Holy

Spirit. He gave the Holy Spirit, as described in John, to the total body so that it is held by the community and is possessed as a property by no one. And in the Book of Acts we see that, because the whole body is possessed, is filled, is sanctified, is transformed and transfigured by the presence of the Holy Spirit, individual members can receive him and be fulfilled – each of them in a unique, unrepeatable and wonderful way.

So again, the Spirit God is present in the Church and our life is 'hid with Christ in God' (Col 3:3), possessed of the Holy Spirit – or, rather, possessed by the Holy Spirit as the Body of Christ, as an extension of his Body through the mysteries of baptism and communion, an extension through participation of his incarnate presence throughout the ages and throughout all lands. The Church is related to the Father in a way which is not metaphorical or allegorical, but which is substantial and real. St Irenaeus of Lyon, speaking of his vision of the future, of what will happen when all things are fulfilled, says to us that the day will come when we, the Body of Christ and the temple of the Holy Spirit, pervaded by the one and at one with the other, will 'in the only begotten Son become the only begotten Son of God'.

This is the vision and this is the incipient reality. It has begun, it is in motion, it is in progress. And this is the divine aspect of the Church, which makes it holy, which makes it *catholic* – not in the sense of an extension through space or even through time, but in the sense of the Greek word which means both 'in all' and 'through all': in each of us to the extent to which we are members, living members of Christ and temples of the Holy Spirit, to the extent to which we are becoming what we already are. In the Church there is a fullness of relationship, there is incipiently the fullness of what Christ was. But there is also, I believe, a human aspect, there is a sinful aspect, as in our unfaithfulness, our disloyalty, our sinfulness. Yet each of us through faith, through love of God, through the loyalty which we do have, however weak, frail, hesitant and even intermittent, is already sharing in the mystery of the Church in its fullness.

In the Church there is the Lord Jesus Christ, truly the Son of God, but also the Son of Man, he who is true Man, both in the sense of being one of us in every single respect except sin, and because he is the only true man, because he is a partaker of the divine nature which is our vocation, according to the words of St Peter (2

Pet 1:4). He is what each of us is called to be. As God-man, he is God by nature and man by nature. We are human by nature and must become divine, transfigured and united to the divine nature by participation. In the Church, he is a revelation to us of what we are called to become. If this is what the Church is, then there is no common measure between it and any kind of 'structure', however wise, however elaborate, however true within its limits and its nature. Because the Church is as vast as God, as big as God, as holy and creatively dynamic as the living God at work within us and in our midst.

Whatever history has offered us in the way of structures, the 'working situations', as it were, in which human beings have had to achieve their vocations, none of these working situations, each of which a scientist would call a 'model', can be accepted as the model of the Church. The only true model of the Church, in the words of the Russian philosopher Nikolai Federov,[49] is the Holy Trinity. The Church must be a drawing near to Trinitarian life, the Church must be a revelation on earth of those relationships of

---

[49] Nikolai Fedorov (1829–1903): Russian Christian philosopher.

oneness in multiplicity which we find in God in his oneness in the Trinity.

The Eucharist does not sum up the Church

That brings me to another point. We have been, and still are, under the sway of a 'eucharistic' theology of the Church which is, I believe, true within limits – though within very narrow limits – but which falsifies our vision if we imagine that it is fully adequate. A eucharistic theology of the Church basically affirms that the Church is the Eucharist and that the Eucharist is the Church, and that those structures which are necessary, which are essential in the eucharistic celebration, are a vision of what constitutes the Church. This means that there must be a presiding minister, and a Church that is structured around him. We are indebted for this profound vision of the Church to the Russian theologian, Father Nikolai Afanasiev,[50] but I do not believe that this is all there is to be said about the Church.

---

[50] Fr Nikolai Afanasiev (1893–1966): influential figure in the Russian emigration, who taught at the St Sergius Theological Institute in Paris.

The Church is greater than the Eucharist, the Church contains the Eucharist, but the Eucharist does not sum up all that there is to the Church. I think we must realise this. Even in eucharistic terms we are easily led astray by what we see. We see a celebrant – be it patriarch, bishop or priest – celebrating, and we watch him until he becomes so central that we may even forget the true event because it is too centred around him. We forget, for instance, that when the priest – whatever his rank may be – has prepared the holy bread and the holy wine, when he is vested and when all the ministers that will take part in the celebration are ready to start, the deacon then addresses himself to the chief celebrant with the words: 'Now it is time for the Lord to act'.

You have done all that is humanly possible; you have prayed and prepared yourself as best as you can to stand face to face with the living God, to come to the place which is like the burning bush, a space which you cannot tread without being cleansed by divine fire; you have vested yourself in vestments that blot out your human personality as far as the celebration is concerned; you have prepared bread and wine and have made the action that follows possible; but the essence of the events is beyond your power, for no one through apostolic succession or functional grace can make a human being capable of turning bread into the Body of Christ, or wine into the Blood of Christ. No human being has the power to force God into any situation, and the only true celebrant of the Eucharist – the only celebrant indeed of any sacrament, that is, of those mighty acts of God which transfigure, and transform the world – is God himself.

The Lord Jesus Christ, because he died and rose again, because he has conquered and sits on the right hand of glory, is the High Priest of creation. He is the only celebrant of every sacrament, while it is the Holy Spirit whom we call upon to come and sanctify the gifts with the certainty that a response of compassion, of love is waiting for us, a response that can transform what is earthly into what is divine. No human being, no earthly being, can make divine what belongs to the earth, and to imagine that the eucharistic structure is an image of the total Church can make us forget that the true celebrant is not the one whom we see before us, but he who is enthroned on the Holy Table, which we call in Orthodox terms, the Throne of God.

So in this sense, the Church is vaster than the Eucharist. Indeed, this is made absolutely clear

in the Eucharist itself, after the communion of
the people, when the priest in a secret prayer
says: 'And grant us, O Lord, to partake more
perfectly of thee in the never-ending day of thy
Kingdom'. There is something greater even
than this – and I do not wish to minimise the
sacredness, the holiness, the greatness, the
importance of the Eucharist. But the Eucharist is
not yet the Church revealed in its fullness even
on earth.

The Thirty-fourth Apostolic Canon

A eucharistic theology tends to lead us inevitably
to the idea of a pyramid of primacies. A priest
celebrates the Eucharist and becomes the *primus*
of the given congregation. The bishop stands at
the head of the clerical body – not the ecclesiastical body, but the clerical one – and then a
greater unity is formed with someone always
standing at the head of the pyramid.

Well, this is not true. Only the Lord Jesus
Christ – and no one else – stands at the head of
the pyramid, whether in a small parish, in a
cathedral church, or in the Church universal.
Whenever we say that someone is the 'Vicar' of

Christ, we say that Christ is absent and that someone is needed to stand in for him. Of course, this is untrue, but our absurd approach to things makes this kind of vocabulary possible. In Orthodoxy as well as Roman Catholicism, there is the same temptation to build a pyramid with someone standing at the top. There was a time when it was Rome, then it became Constantinople – but it could be anyone. And it would be as false, because there is no one save the Lord Jesus Christ who stands there, who has a right to stand there and who is actually standing here.

So when we speak of 'primacy' and 'primacies' we must realise that we are at a point of tension between history and theology. This becomes clear when we consider a remarkable statement contained in what we call the Thirty-fourth Apostolic Canon. I say 'what we call' because, quite definitely, it was not coined by the Apostles. It is called 'apostolic' because the Church's consciousness has recognised in it something rooted in the apostolic approach and way of doing things.

This Apostolic Canon states that 'it behoves the bishops of every nation to know the one among them who is their chief, and to recognise him as their head, and to refrain from doing anything beyond their own territory or function without his advice and approval; but, instead, each of them should do only whatever is needed by his own parish or territory; but let not even such a one [i.e. their chief] do anything without the advice and consent and approval of all. For thus there will be concord, and God will be glorified through the Lord in the Holy Spirit, Father, Son and Holy Spirit.'

This is an extremely interesting canon, because its conclusion is that it is in the harmony of the parts and the totality of multiplicity that God is glorified. And here we must remember that 'to glorify' in Greek does not mean what we understand so often – to praise or applaud; it means that his splendour, his unutterable beauty is revealed. The root of Canon 34 is this: our purpose in history, despite our frailty and our sinfulness, is to reveal something of the unity of God in three persons. It can be revealed by concord, by unanimity, by the fact that the many in God's own name can become one in a perfect harmony of will and action. To demonstrate this – and this is the point at which theology becomes history, when vision becomes action – there must be units in which this unity in multiplicity is demonstrated by the fact that one will act as a father and the other as a son, that the son will turn to the father with confidence, with love, with respect, but that never will the father act with power, or in an arbitrary way, but in unanimity and concord with the other.

Here, perhaps, it is worth remarking on the difference there is between authority and power. Power consists in the ability of a given person, or group of persons, to enforce its will and its decisions upon others. Authority is something quite different. In a sense authority has no power; it is the persuasiveness of truth that is authority.

I would like to quote here from the introduction which Hans Kung wrote to Hasler's book on the infallibility of the Pope:

The first Ecumenical Council of Nicea (325) got along without any claim to infallibility. Recent historical research has pointed out the way in which the leader of this Council, Athanasius, along with many Greek Fathers of the Church and Augustine as well, explained the true but in no sense infallible authority of a council. A council speaks the truth not because it is convoked in a juridical and unobjectionable manner, not because the majority of bishops in the world were in attendance, not because it was confirmed by any sort of human authority, not, in a word, because it was, from the start, incapable of being deceived; but because, in spite of new words it says nothing new, because it hands on the old tradition in a new language, because it bears witness to the original message, because it breathes the air of Scripture, because it has the Gospel behind it.

This is, I would think, the difference between authority and power. Power means – as 'Vatican I' had proclaimed, despite the number of bishops who walked out of it and said 'no' to infallibility – that a certain thing is so and that one has either to accept it or be rejected. But what we see in the first Ecumenical Council is no act of power. And all that we have received throughout history from the Ecumenical Councils has been a voice sounding from the depth of the scriptures, indeed, God's own voice, the voice of the Holy Spirit proclaiming what is true, what can be recognised as truth by the Church. It has been recognised as true by the Church because of the perfect harmony which was perceived between the original, primeval word of God and what resounded from these Councils, between the word of the Spirit and the words of men. It was the beauty of this harmony which was the convincing power of their proclamation of the Truth.

Recapturing the spirit of the early Church

We are now in a situation in which the Thirty-fourth Apostolic Canon can have new meaning for us. The historical primacies, those great conglomerations which history has created, are breaking down and gradually falling to pieces – thanks be to God. We are gradually losing the forms which were built as images of the political states of Rome, Byzantium and other countries. The Russian Church is a sad example in this respect because our Patriarchate is so vast, so monolithic and so monarchical in the way in which it acts, that it is very difficult to recapture the spirit of the early Church. And yet this vision of the Church as God the Holy Trinity mirrored – and, indeed more than mirrored: alive, dynamic, living – in the Church is not something that can be seen. It must be demonstrated. And it can be demonstrated, but only in a small unit where everyone knows everyone, where people know and respect each other, in small dioceses where everyone is known to the bishop and the bishop is known to the priests. (And this will not always be an advantage for him, because he will be known not only as the bishop, but as the miserable creature he may be on occasion.) The Church must exist in units that are small enough to be visible and comprehended. This is what I believe primacy and primacies are to become in the whole Church. In a way it is achieved much better by a Methodist Superintendent who is responsible for a small circle of people than by an immense Patriachate in which the Patriarch is just perhaps a photograph seen in a calendar and nothing else: a name proclaimed and an illusion that somehow he is 'the boss'.

I would prefer not to end on such a sad note, but I do think we must pray that this theological vision of the Church should find a real, concrete, intense expression in the concord that exists within units where concord makes sense. There is no possible concord between a parishioner in Irkutsk and the Patriarch of Moscow except on the assumption that whatever the Patriarch says is right – or an underlying feeling that he is probably wrong, but nothing can be done against him. We must recapture this theological vision and turn it into a demonstration of the truth. One can, for administrative or practical reasons, have something bigger, but it is not this that will correspond to the Thirty-fourth Apostolic Canon. It is not this that will eventually correct, first in the consciousness of the people and then in the practice of the Church, the terrible results of the misinterpretation of Canon 3 of Constantinople concerning the two 'primacies', results that have gradually spread like weeds to other areas of the Church.

Finally, I would like to say that in order to achieve this we must become more Christian than we are, must be more in Christ and in the Spirit. And we must also recapture a theology of primacy which is true, because one cannot on false premises build a vision of the true Church.

PART IV

❦ ❦

Orthodox Christianity
in the World

8

※ ❦

The Russian Church

This talk was given at St Basil's House, in London, then the headquarters of the Fellowship of St Alban and St Sergius, on 14 November 1984.

I feel that there are a certain number of basic things which must be understood about the Russian Church in order to understand it not superficially, not on the level of news, but in its deeper substance.

When Christianity came to Russia it did not meet a mythological religion as developed and as elaborate as those it had met in Western Europe. Greek mythology, Greek philosophical thought, the faith of the Western pagan nations, was a great deal more intellectually refined and elaborate than that of the Slavs, and particularly the Russian Slavs. So the confrontation between two intellectual currents, between two religious experiences, did not result either in a fusion or in a clash. Christianity came to a nation that, as far as we know from ancient documents and from research, had a sense of God, had a pagan vision of God, but no mythology and no philosophy that would elaborate on it. So it was the meeting of living human souls that had perceived God in the way they could, thought of God in the way that was accessible to them from their experience of nature, of themselves, of man, of circumstances, and it gave a form and a meaning to things which were more or less vaguely perceived.

The result was that Christianity in Russia did not take first of all an intellectual form. It did not reach Russia with all the richness which Byzantium possessed at the moment when Byzantine, and indirectly through them, Bulgarian missionaries reached Russia. Christianity was discovered in a more direct and overwhelming manner. What we know from the chronicles is that Prince Vladimir,[51] under the influence of his grandmother, Princess Olga, who was one of the

---

[51] Saint Vladimir Svyatoslavich the Great (c. 958–1015): grand prince of Kiev who converted to Christianity in 988.

very first Christians in Russia, sent emissaries to
find out about other religions. Not only had he
perceived something in the vision of God which
his grandmother possessed, but he already had
presumably, from what we know of his life
afterwards, perceived that the religion of his
father and of his surroundings was not sufficient
for him. He was hungry for something that was
deeper, truer, more real. He sent emissaries to
investigate the religions of the Jews and of the
Muslims, and also south, because this was
the great commercial road of Russian history,
to Byzantium. The chronicles tell us the story
of this visit in an anecdotal form. They tell
us that the emissaries that went to investigate
the Jewish religion came and told Prince
Vladimir what they had learned and also that
the Jews were in dispersion because they
were under the wrath of God. And Vladimir is
said to have reacted to it by saying: 'That is a
religion which I do not want to embrace. I do not
want to have a quarrel with God before I have
even embraced a religion.' He found out also
that the Muslims forbade the drinking of spirits,
and said that that was no religion for a Slav, or a
Russian. So he was reduced to turning to
Christianity.

The emissaries that went to Byzantium did not come with a system of theological thought. What they reported to him was that while they were standing in the great cathedral of Saint Sophia in Constantinople they did not know whether they were on earth or in heaven. What they perceived was the unutterable beauty of the act of worship. What they perceived was the awe and the faith of the people. And this was the beginning of Russian Christianity, the perception of surpassing beauty. You may remember, because you are probably more cultured than our Russian ancestors, that Plato had said that beauty is the convincing power of truth. Anything to which we cannot respond by saying, 'How beautiful!' has not reached our soul. If we say only, 'It must be true; yes, it is true', and perceive it only with our cold and sober intellect, we have not yet identified with the truth. It is only when it is beauty that the truth flowers up in us.

This, then, was the first and basic perception of the Russians: Christianity as beauty, Christianity as worship, and a worship that was full of awe and at the same time full of tenderness; a God that was the God of Heaven, but also was the God who had come to earth and in an act of love had become one of us, a God who had become accessible, a God who had a name – I was about to say a Christian name – a human name, a God whom one could approach, calling him Jesus, and not only the Holy One of Israel or the Almighty or any of these great and awe-inspiring, frightening titles. This has remained a feature of Russian Orthodoxy throughout the ages. One of the expressions which one found in popular speech about someone who had become a Christian at heart and not an intellectual Christian, someone who had become an Orthodox with a sense of the unutterable greatness of God and his even more unutterable closeness, the expression was, 'He carries Christ in his bosom', meaning under his coat, as it were, close to his heart.

So Russia's first experience of Christianity was of worship and beauty, of the greatness of God, of a God who was so great that he could become as small as he wanted without being diminished by his descent from the throne of heaven to the level of man. He was one of us, yet he remained himself. And, further, by becoming one of us he showed us something about ourselves which we could not possibly have discovered, and something about himself which we would never have dared think about. What he made us discover is that man, the concrete man whom everyone knew in his frailty, in his sinfulness, to be a prisoner of evil and at the same time open to the greatest good, was not only capable of being spirit-bearing but capable of being God-bearing. Our humanity was such that God himself could become man without ceasing to be God. It was a revelation that man was so great, so mysteriously deep, so totally mysterious that God and man could become one, and that if it had happened once in Christ, by participating in the mystery of Christ – by becoming, through the mysteries of the Church, members, living cells of his body – we could become what he was: sons, daughters by adoption, but not in a situation of adopted children who for ever feel that they are not the children of the family, but children who enter into this divine and human family by an act that integrates them, but once they are integrated, for ever become truly sons and daughters of the Most High.

All this came to Russia later with patristic writings, with the liturgical texts that are imbued with this experience, but it was there as a germinal experience, as a direct experience of the soul through truth revealed as beauty and adoration. And then, something was disclosed already then

about God, God whom the Christian countries
had known for a thousand years, on whom they
had reflected: a God who, while remaining the
unfathomable God of Heaven, revealed himself
as the God of the Incarnation, but through his
Incarnation revealed to us that he was the Lamb
of God slain before all worlds, that he was by
choice and by an act of will, in an act of love for
us, vulnerable, given, helpless, because he had
chosen to identify himself with us. And this
revealed to the early Slavs of Russia the significance and the value of all mankind. If God
could come so low, if God could identify himself
with us, with our condition, without first claim-
ing that we should become different, then what
was man?

Vladimir had led a life which in the elegant,
euphemistic terms of the liturgical texts is compared to that of Solomon. If any of you is
familiar with the Bible, you will remember that
Solomon had an innumerable number of concubines and wives, and that his form of life was
not the ideal which one would wish to see in a
God-established king. So was also Vladimir. The
first response of Vladimir to this vision of God
and this vision of man was a total change of life.
His life and his attitude to man, to his subjects,

changed radically in two particular ways. On the one hand, instead of feeling that he was simply the ruler, he felt that he was responsible for his people. And we find in the Kiev of the ninth century, in an extraordinary manner, an embryo welfare state. Kiev was a small town or a big village in those days. But every day tables were prepared in the court of Vladimir's palace with food for the poor. Anyone could come and eat. And those people who were too old or infirm to come had food delivered on carts drawn by oxen that went round the city and brought it to the sick and the old. This was his response to the Gospel – concrete and simple. And I think these two qualities, these two characteristics, have remained characteristics of Russian piety: Russian theology understood as knowledge and worship of God, and the social consciousness of Russia.

There is no time to trace this through history, but let me give you two examples. Later, in the time of Ivan the Terrible and immediately afterwards, there lived a nobleman, Joseph of Volokolamsk. He collected around him a vast number of monks, about a thousand, who all came from what we now call the upper classes. He submitted them to the most fierce ascetic discipline in northern or central Russia, which from our point of view is very far north. They were allowed to wear only one piece of clothing summer and winter, and never had any fire in their cells. The rules of fasting were rigorous, and they had to work desperately hard. But their desperately hard work produced nothing for their own benefit. It was done to feed the population that surrounded them. And at a certain moment when a famine struck them, Joseph of Volokolamsk commanded the barns to be opened and the wheat and all food to be distributed, and his monks said to him, 'But we are starving'. And he said, 'Yes, we are, but we have chosen to starve. They haven't.' And the food was given.

We find the same concern for the poor and needy in the person of John of Kronstadt,[52] or of a number of other ascetics or priests or indeed lay people in the nineteenth century. So this runs like a golden thread throughout Russian history: the sense of beauty, the sense of adoration based

---

[52] John of Kronstadt (1829–1908), priest of the Russian Church, renowned for his works of charity. He was canonised by ROCOR in 1964, and by the Russian Orthodox Church in 1990.

on awe, love, exhilaration at the vision of this beauty, this concern for one's fellow human beings.

But something else also occurred. The change from paganism to Christianity was a sudden event. It was like moving from darkness into light, from death into life, or – to use an image which belongs to C. S. Lewis – the difference between a believer and an unbeliever is the same as exists between a statue and a living body. The statue may be very beautiful, the living person far less, but the one is of stone, immobile, dead, inactive, while the other is creative and alive. And this is what happened to those who embraced the Christian faith. They had been in existence, and they came to life. They had been a potentiality, and they became reality. They had been engulfed in that stream of divine life that poured upon the world on the day of Pentecost. But this could not be contained selfishly. It could not be possessed simply in order to enjoy it. Those who have been unbelievers and discover God at a certain moment of their life know very well the absolute difference that it makes, and that it is impossible to contain the exhilaration of it. It must be shared because one cannot allow anyone to go through life without sharing the miracle which has given life to the one who has discovered God and become a participant of his life, and so from the very beginning we find missionaries in the Russian Church.

It is a sort of commonplace to think of the Russian Church as never having had any real missions. Indeed when you compare Russia and its missionary work to the West you do not see Russian missionaries leaving their country and going into the new world: the Americas, Australia and so forth. But if you look at the map of Russia and realise that from this little city of Kiev Christianity spread throughout this immense territory, you realise the extent of the missionary work that took place.

Now when you try to be a missionary on your own territory, it is difficult because everyone knows you, and does not think of you as someone who has fallen from heaven, unknown, someone whom one discovers only through his words and his message, but as someone one has known for donkey's years as being in his past greedy or lazy or evil. So it is a much more difficult thing to convert anyone when the one can say, 'Look here, I have known you so well. Don't tell me that you have discovered something great. You couldn't contain it.'

The fact is that the missionary work was done by two kinds of people. There were those who made an attempt at going to those who knew nothing of Christ to bring to them the joy and glory and wonder of what they had discovered themselves. Such were St Kuksha[53] in the early days, and St Stephen of Perm,[54] who went to the region of Perm, learned the language of the people, invented an alphabet for them, translated for them basic passages from the Scriptures and from the books of prayer and brought Christianity to them. There is a very interesting passage in his life, which is quoted by Fedotov in his book on Russian saints and which exists in the original Slavonic text. The local witch-doctors and priests found themselves in competition with the new missionary and, having engaged in argument with him and being defeated felt they must get rid of him somehow. And so they sent

[53] Saint Kuksha (d. 1113): a priest-monk at the Monastery of the Kievan Caves. He left Kiev for what is now the Orel region of Russia in order to undertake pioneering missionary work, in the course of which he was martyred.

[54] St Stephen of Perm (1340–96). First bishop of Perm and founder of the Permian written tradition. Rather than imposing Latin or Church Slavonic on the indigenous pagan population, as contemporary missionaries did, Stephen learned their language and traditions and worked out a writing system for their use.

three or four men to murder him. They came back without having done so. And when they were asked whether they had done it, they said: 'We came to kill him, and he received us with such love that we simply knelt down and asked for his blessing.'

This was the way in which Christianity gradually progressed. I do not mean to say that there were not bad or miserable sides to the missionary work of the Russian Church, particularly later, when missionaries were sent out and when the populations discovered that there were worldly, temporal advantages in being Christian and integrated into the greater Russian community. But this was the impetus.

Then there was another kind of missionary, not people who went out to meet the pagan but those who ran away from the veneration of their own fellow Christians. This is the way in which Christianity reached Alaska, which then was Russian territory. A man called German, a monk of the Valamo monastery, became known, revered, celebrated, surrounded with admiration, and he decided to go. So he left and moved around the north of Russia. He settled after a while, and having settled, he began to pray and to lead a monastic life. He was discovered by a hunter who was impressed by his face and who talked about him. Others came, and after a while German found that life had again become noisy, and again he moved on. And moving on, away and away and away from vanity and the admiration of people, he reached the Bering Strait, which means about 5000 miles across Siberia and northern Russia. And there he found an expanse of water with little islands and land on the other side, and he felt that that was the end of the world. He crossed, and there he found the Aleutians, and he became their first missionary. And he felt he could not go further. And he died there, having created a first centre of Christianity.

The same kind of thing happened also with Nicholas of Japan,[55] who was canonised in recent years. In 1864, he went to Japan. Before that he had been a student in a theological school, and a call reached it for a student to volunteer to become the chaplain to the embassy in Tokyo. He thought it had nothing to do with him and continued on his usual activities, but in the evening when he prayed he suddenly felt that

---

[55] Nicholas of Japan (1836–1912).

it was a direct call to him by God. He volunteered, was sent to Japan, and there he decided first of all to learn Japanese. He must have had a colossal ability to work: he had two teachers because he wore one out in the course of half a day, and so they succeeded one another. And so the two men pumped Japanese into him. One was a priest, a Shintoist priest, and the other was a Samurai, a warrior. When he had acquired enough knowledge of Japanese, he began to have, of course, religious conversations and theological arguments. The priest listened and argued. The soldier was incensed, seeing that his faith was challenged, and he smote Nikolai in the face. Nikolai bowed down to the ground and said 'Forgive me for having angered you' and the man was so profoundly shaken by his humility and his love and by the way he had been able to receive, to accept the humiliation of the blow that he began to look into Christianity in a new way and he became, eventually, together with the priest, one of the two first missionaries of Nikolai of Japan. When Nikolai died, I think he left 35,000 Christians behind him and a number of clergy.

In a way he is particularly close to the Fellowship[56] in that he left his *panagia*[57] to his successor Sergei Tychomirov, who made a present of it to the English writer Birkbeck. And the English writer Birkbeck made a present of it to Nicholas Zernov.[58] When I came into the Fellowship almost thirty-six years ago, I discovered the *panagia* lying in the chapel, took a glance, and saw what it was because there was a note attached to it. And I thought, 'I must take it away because I am sure that one day an honoured visitor who will care nothing for the object will come and be given this *panagia* as a memento of his visit to the Fellowship.' So I hid it on the top shelf behind books. Some years later it was decided that I should be made a bishop, so I turned to the Fellowship with a plea. Could I be allowed to wear this *panagia* for my consecration, as a blessing from Nikolai of Japan and a

---

[56] The Fellowship of St Alban and St Sergius (Anglican–Orthodox Fellowship), to whom this talk was given. As a young priest, Metropolitan Anthony was Chaplain to the Fellowship from 1948 to 1950 – his first assignment in England before becoming rector of the Russian Orthodox parish in London, and founder of the Diocese of Sourozh.

[57] Image of the Mother of God worn by a bishop alongside his priest's cross.

[58] Nicholas Zernov (1898–1980): lay theologian and founder member of the Fellowship of St Alban and St Sergius.

blessing from the Fellowship, who had invited me in the first place to come to this country for a period of two years. That has expanded now to thirty-five plus. The *panagia* was not where they had left it. It was not there. No one knew where it was – except me! And the Fellowship was so generous as to give me this *panagia* as a blessing instead of allowing me only to wear it on that occasion. And this is the *panagia* which I wear and which I treasure so much.

Now there is a problem which has been there in the course of all Russian history. It is the relationship between Church and State, between the Christian world of Russia and the State in Russia. This problem has evolved in a variety of ways. To begin with, in the case of Vladimir and in the early days of Christianity, it was the Church that was the mind and the spirit of the Russian nation. But of course it did not prevent sin, evil, violence, as it did not prevent those things in any of the countries in which Christianity has taken root throughout the world. But there was this longing for the perfect harmony and beauty all the same.

Later on a succession of things happened. The first was around the period of Ivan the Terrible, of his predecessor and successor. The State had

to become the protector, the military protector
of the nation against the Tartar invasion, and
therefore acquired an identity that could not
simply overlap with the Church. The Church had
another function. And gradually the awareness
of having an identity distinct from that of the
Church came to the fore. Then we discover a
new type of saintliness in Russia: the fools for
Christ's sake. They appear at the same time and
under the same conditions as they appeared in
Constantinople. The moment the State began to
become secular and to have its own values –
earthly values, political and social, distinct from
the Gospel – these men and women appeared
who counterfeited mental illness and whose
behaviour in every respect was a mockery, a
ridiculing of all the values that were purely
human as distinct from divine. They dressed,
they ate, they moved, they acted in ways that
were offensive to all well-behaved, law-abiding
citizens. And they rejected in their behaviour, in
their apparent folly, the thing which we humans
treasure above all: our mind, our brain. We
always feel that this is our most precious characteristic. We can think. We are possessed of
reason. And that they rejected. There are many
stories about them, but in the course of the next

150 years, as the State was asserting itself against the Church, not in opposition but in separation, the fools for Christ's sake stood there saying: 'Folly, folly, folly, all your secular way is folly and nothing else.' And this is a phenomenon which again we find also in Byzantium and to a certain extent also in the West, in France and in other countries.

Later on with the Revolution, a new situation occurred. Church and State were no longer two entities living side by side and interpenetrating one another to a greater or lesser extent. They were two entities of which one was aggressively opposed to the other, determined to destroy the other, not only as a structure and an organisation, but in its very substance, its inner self. And the Church was confronted with the problem of its attitude to this. The choice which was made by the Church is very much misunderstood, I believe, and in order to try to make it clear, I will begin by quoting someone who is beyond criticism from that angle – the German pastor Martin Niemoller. You may know that Niemoller was the head of the confessing Church in Germany, of that part of the church in Germany that took a stand against the national socialist movement and stood firm and rejected it. He came to this country, I think a few more than thirty years ago, and spoke to a meeting of the German clergy, and so it was not for my benefit that he said what I will repeat now. He said at a certain point: 'There is one thing which I cannot forgive myself for. It never occurred to me during this struggle that our persecutors were the lost sheep of the fold of Christ and were my own charges.' And he added: 'This is what the Russian Church has not done.' And this impressed me very much, because if anyone had a right to accuse the Russian Church of being in the wrong, he had the right to do this. What the Russian Church has felt is what Patriarch Alexis [I] defined by saying: 'The Church is the Body of Christ broken for the salvation of the world, for the salvation, not against the salvation, not against the world.' And the Church from the very beginning has accepted to be broken, to be a crucified Church, to be a persecuted Church, to be a Church in fetters – and at the same time a Church which considers itself responsible not only for its members but for the persecutors, for its enemies, for those who wish to destroy it. In fact the division between the believing world and the unbelieving world is as complex in Russia as it is in all the extreme situations. It is complex because the demarcation line between believers, or at least practising Christians, and the unbelieving or non-practising Christians cuts right across the family. What Christ said – two against three and three against two – is true. And you find that in the same family some members are believers and some are not. This creates a knot which ties together, links and unites together people, the unbeliever and the believer. How can a mother curse her unbelieving son? How can the unbelieving son wish the destruction of a body while the mother is a living limb of this body? And so the situation is of a complexity which I cannot describe because I do not live within it.

The Church has been oppressed or persecuted in a variety of ways at different times. There has been the bloodshed of the early days. There has been administrative oppression since. And there are all the time tensions and difficulties which vary very much with the local situation. You realise that Russia is extremely big and that as a rule, the farther you are from a centre the better. That is why schoolboys like to sit at the back of a class rather than the front near their teacher. And also in each region there is a state representative in charge of Church affairs, and a lot depends on him. Some are law-abiding. In other words, they try to be sure that the law is applied, and some consider that the law is only the letter and the spirit says destroy and destroy down to the foundations. So that creates a very motley situation. We have an increasing number of young people. One interesting development is that recently graduates from the university have become able to study theology, which was absolutely out of the question before, and which will gradually make a great deal of difference to the type of clergy we have and to their intellectual and theological level.

There is also, I think, the fact that the Church is the only body that is a non-Soviet body. Every other body is a state organisation to one degree or another. The Church is not. Oppressed, limited, controlled, infiltrated to a certain extent, spied upon, it still is the only body which has got its own ideology, which is incompatible with materialism and which has survived. And the fact that nowadays the Church does exist is practically a certainty of survival, because if it was not destroyed at the moment when there were perhaps a thousand churches in the whole of Russia, when terror, in the Lenin–Stalin period, was rife, then there seems to be no possibility of ultimate destruction. There is another phenomenon also, that contact of the Soviet state with the West, and the world at large, has made it necessary or possible for certain values to be brought into the picture: for instance, the Helsinki agreement about human rights. However badly applied it may be in Soviet Russia, it is still there as an undertaking by the Soviet state. It can be referred to. And there are a number of representatives of the secular society and of the Church who base their action for freedom on these agreements. In that sense contacts with the West have proved a help and important. What I believe is very important is understanding and support rather than criticism from the height of one's freedom and dignity.

❦❦

9

The Orthodox Church in Diaspora: A Reply to Syndesmos

Founded in 1953, Syndesmos, the World Fellowship of Orthodox Youth, is a federation of Orthodox youth movements and theological schools around the world, working under the blessing of all the local canonical Churches. Delegates at the third Syndesmos Orthodox Youth Festival held in Spetses, in August 1988, wrote to the bishops of the Orthodox Church expressing their concerns about many aspects of Church life. The full text of the letter can be found on the Syndesmos website at http://www.syndesmos.org/content/en/texts/files/Text_ 88%20Letter%20to%20the%20bishops,%20Spetses,% 201988.pdf. In particular, they raised the question of the many jurisdictional divisions and how a divided Church could witness to unity, as well as raising questions about communications, the role of women, mission, ethical teaching and the Church's witness in the world. The reply written by Metropolitan Anthony and his clergy was published in Syndesmos News, 1991, Vol. IX, No. 1.

The Russian Orthodox Church
67 Ennismore Gardens
London SW7 1NH

Dear Members of Syndesmos,

This response to your *Letter to the Bishops of the Orthodox Church*, is long overdue; the reason for the delay lies in the fact that our Diocese wanted to study it carefully and involve in the process both the Clergy and the Laity of Sourozh, that is, the members of the Russian Orthodox Diocese of Great Britain and Ireland.

We are happy to see that young Orthodox of all countries are taking the initiative and challenging the Hierarchy of our Church on matters which transcend the concerns of any of the National Churches. Our National Churches 'at home' are not and cannot be sufficiently aware of the multinational situation of Orthodoxy in the Diaspora; they need both the testimony and the challenge which can be offered only from within the Orthodox Dispersion. Thank you for taking a first step in this direction.

In the name of the Diocese of Sourozh, that is, in the name of the Laity, the Presbytery and in my own name, I now offer the following comments to your letter.

We all tend to think of resolving problems in terms of organisation, of establishing structures. This is a mistake. It is life that can create forms; structures must express life and be supple enough and fluid enough to vary according to local situations and real needs; even the Canons of the Church are yardsticks and precedents to be learned from, not immutable rules intended to force life into obsolete patterns; they were legitimate for situations which no longer exist but now need a new vision. This is the way in which the Canons were gradually framed; some express the very being of the Church, some were intended to meet concrete situations which no longer exist. We must, all of us, look deeply into the concrete situation in which we live and ask ourselves what is God's will for us here and now, learn to discern the promptings of the Spirit of God, and discern God's activity in our own time and place. Structures cannot create the visible unity of the Orthodox Church any more than diplomatic agreements can bring together divided Christians. One does not build unity, one grows into it, by adhering ever more completely and perfectly to the Gospel and giving to things temporal, ethnic, cultural, national, their legitimate, yet secondary place.

We must recognise the fact that the Orthodox are divided on more than on level; to love one's language, one's culture, one's heritage is legitimate: to reject others who do not share it and cling to their own treasures is not. The younger generation is in danger of either clinging to the past of their families, or trying to create new ethnic forms and so ceasing to be what their parents were, in order to become members of the secular society in which they live. Creating new ethnicities in order to break down barriers is no solution – this would add one more problem to those that already exist.

Special consideration should be given to the schisms which have their origin in the political upheavals of the last century; the generation which is yours does not know from direct experience how and why they occurred. It is easy to condemn those responsible for them and their present heirs and followers, but think of the tragic destinies of the generation of your own parents and grandparents and their contemporaries; think of all they lost, of all they endured and then you may understand why they seceded from their Mother Churches and formed temporary ecclesiastic administrations (or jurisdictions) which have survived till now and have begun to appear as obsolete to their members themselves. With a change of political climate in Russia and other countries, and a greater openness and understanding by all parties concerned (I am thinking of the Old Believers in Russia and abroad, of the Old Calendarists in Greece and elsewhere, of the schism between the Serbian Patriarchate and the Church in Macedonia and others), ways must be found to recognise one another. An offer was made a few years ago by the Patriarchate of Moscow to the Russian Church in Exile [i.e. ROCOR] to re-establish communion in prayer and sacraments while retaining administrative independence and without any change in political stance being expected. This new openness is gradually bearing fruit.

You seem to dislike the term 'Diaspora'; it describes accurately the state of affairs: Orthodox people of different nationalities happen to live in all the countries of the world as a religious minority, with a varying degree of scatteredness – in some places as individuals, in others as small or relatively big parishes, too distant from one another to maintain contact; in other places small or larger dioceses in the midst of much more numerous non-Orthodox bodies, always too small and also still too ethnic to be one of the denominations of the country where they live. Yet there is another dimension to being a Diaspora, a positive one. The dominant position of our Churches in the countries from which we come and their close association with the State have accustomed us to think in terms totally alien to early Christians in terms of what one often calls 'the gathered community': yet the vocation of the Church is to bring the Gospel to all creatures, to be like a handful of seed which the Master of the harvest scatters far and wide, so that it brings fruit in all places where even one seed falls. Berdyaev[59] wrote a very beautiful article on the subject in the early years of our Russian exile – telling us that we were sent by God into the whole world to bring Orthodoxy to those who had lost it and needed it; the Apostles, twelve men, and the comparatively few disciples did not stay cooped up together; they parted from one another to bring the Good News to those who sat in darkness. Though distant from each other, they knew that they were one, because they all were in Christ, and doing the work he had sent them to do. This is a true meaning of 'Diaspora': to be a mission, a band of

[59] Nikolai Berdyaev (1874–1948): Christian existentialist philosopher and leading figure of the first Russian emigration.

witnesses. To do this we need hardly any structures – only a keen fellowship between us all and a sincere, earnest dedication to the service of God. In this context differences of language, of culture, of ethnicity, are no impediments; they only enrich the message, make it more human, more accessible in its rich variety to all those who receive it.

It is our clinging to structures that divides us; the multiplicity of national jurisdictions would not separate us if no jurisdiction claimed superiority over others, rights of power instead of the privilege of serving more faithfully than others, if co-operation in all things was the rule. We still need bishops and clergy who speak national languages to serve those who have not yet acquired a common language with other Orthodox living in the same territory; we must cherish our languages, as both prayers, spiritual writings and theological statements often cannot be translated adequately and need living interpreters. We must be deeply rooted in our culture in order to appreciate, assess and share the culture of others. However, we have no right to claim any superiority for our own heritage, but a deep knowledge of it enables us to share its riches with all those who can be enriched by it.

Structures are, of course, necessary to keep together those who share the same heritage, to inspire them to act from within a common and shared experience, for the life of the Sacraments, etc., but they are not an aim in themselves. And least of all should they be seen or used as levers of power. There are a number of structures of oppression in our Church; we forget too easily that the one who is highest is the servant of all, not the overlord. Least of all should the Church face the surrounding world from a position of power, neither should the Church face it from one of subservience. In all human relations the Church is to be the conscience of the world, of every, of any society; speaking the truth in charity, but clearly, without ambiguity, without calculation, daring to criticise or to approve of things without regard to persons and without considering the danger it may involve for herself. Together with all men we must co-operate in the building of the city of man, but adding to the building a dimension which we alone can add – a dimension of depth, of width, of holiness that would allow the only true man – our Lord Jesus Christ, true man and true God – to be its First Citizen; a city of man co-extensive with the City of God. Every Christian must make concrete choices that may be at variance with those of others, yet all must aim at one and the same thing – not at creating a liveable society, but a city so truly human that it may become truly divine.

Building the City of God means giving ourselves to God – discarding both our strength and our weakness and allowing God's grace to act freely in and through us; this is missionary work, but not proselytism. Not an attempt at making others as we are, but sharing with them the transfiguring joy of knowing God and communing with him, so that they may become themselves, as unlike us as they are unique in the eyes of God. It is not in uniformity that we can be one but in the oneness that is attainable only through uniqueness, like musical notes capable of forming one perfect accord because they are themselves, without confusion but also without competition.

I have mentioned the existence of structures of oppression creating distinctions and establishing false hierarchies of value. One is blatantly offensive and must be broken down: it is the position of women in the Church. The Orthodox Church has made more than one unwarranted statement on the subject but has not yet even begun to think about it; the problem is considered as external to us, coming from those Churches that have 'lost their way'. This is untrue; it is at the heart of our Church's life. It must be thought out and seen with new eyes; to be referred to the tradition is not enough, a tradition the meaning of which or whose origin cannot be traced is no tradition, but traditionalism – a superstitious survival of prejudices and misapprehensions. It is for your generation from within the Gospel and the Faith given us by God in Christ to confront these evils.

Other problems are to be faced and resolved: our relationship with the Oriental Orthodox Churches, with whom we share the same faith while we express it in different ways – who will triumph? Those who assess the spirit of these Churches or those who cling to the letter?

Other matters intrinsic to our Church must be examined: whom must we admit to baptism? To integration into the Orthodox Church? Who should be allowed to be married in Church? How should we receive converts? Are we prepared to live our faith or only to speak of it? This raises all the problems of Christian ethics; one can be a heretic in action while professing every iota of it in words if our life gives the lie to our proclamation. Fasting and the ascetical life, the conditions and frequency of Communion; the ways in which religious education must be re-thought to cease to be information and become setting on fire; and many local problems are and will be your responsibility. According to the way you solve them Orthodoxy may become one of the many irrelevant denominations or faiths of the world or its light and inspiration.

It is for you to choose, and to act both daringly and humbly.

May God's blessing and power be in and without.

[Signed]

Metropolitan of Sourozh together with the Clergy and Laity of the Diocese.

10

❧ ❦

Christian Witness in a
Secular State

*This talk looks at the ways in which Christians have borne
witness to the Gospel over the centuries and also touches
on some of the issues raised by tradition and structure
within the Church.*

Twelve Apostles went out into the world in the
power of the Holy Spirit. They were surrounded
by a small group of disciples, in all seventy men
and women. And they converted the world – not
immediately, but they started a wave of understanding, of knowledge, of newness of life, that
made the whole world different from what it
had been for thousands of years before. There
are now millions of Christians of different denominations and yet, because of us Christians,
Christianity seems to become increasingly
irrelevant.

There is a vast society which lives, acts, thinks,

creates, in a world that seemingly has nothing to do with the Gospel. I said 'seemingly', because this is not totally true. The principles on which even godless societies are built very often have Christian roots. Christianity has brought into the world a notion that did not exist in antiquity: the absolute, final value of the person, of every single being. In the past there were masters and slaves. Now there are human beings, men, women, children, each of us unique – and each of us, even though we may not always know it, has an absolute value and significance in the eyes of God, and even in the eyes of society. And yet, somehow we have become irrelevant. I am not challenging you. I am not criticising the Church. But I think there are a number of things which we should reflect on, and see where we stand with regard to them.

The first generation of Christians, the Apostles, the disciples and those who were converted by them, were on a pilgrimage. It was not a sedentary society. The first Christians were people who moved from place to place bringing to others the unutterable joy of a new life in Christ and in the Holy Spirit. On the other hand, those who settled in one place were not an introverted society, a society locked in upon itself, but a society of people who looked outward for the lost sheep of the Kingdom of God. This is something we have lost. All the Churches, in one way or another, have had missions. But what is striking is that far too often the missionaries went out into the world with a sense of offensive, insulting, arrogant superiority. They went into the world in order to give what they possessed, without realising that they possessed nothing, that all they could do was to follow St Paul, who, seeing the vastness, the incredible difficulty of his mission, turned to God for strength. And the Lord said to him: 'My grace suffices unto thee; my strength deploys itself in thy weakness' (2 Cor 12:9). And the tiny group of believers, of Christians, who went into the world following Christ's command 'Go, and bring the Gospel to all nations' (Matt 28:19), they knew that they were frail, defenceless, and that they could not count on any strength except that of God. St Paul said that he would glory in nothing but his weakness, so that everything that happened should be an act of God. This, very often, was not the attitude of Christian missionaries. The missionary movement in Christianity is not generally a movement of people who so love their neighbour with the love of God that they go out to the world ready to die that others may live, who go out into the world, with all the frailty that is theirs, knowing that they can do nothing, but God can do everything.

What some missionaries brought, however, was not the Gospel, not the joy of a new life, not a meeting with the living God. But what is re-markable, even unique, in the preaching of the early missionaries, the Apostles, is that they speak of their experience. One may say, 'They had been with Christ, they could speak of what they saw in him', but this is not the whole truth, because thousands of people met Christ on the roads of the Holy Land, but very few saw him. Their eyes were blind. They saw an outer form, they heard strange, puzzling, even shocking, challenging words, but not words that touched their inner core and made them into new beings. When Christ spoke of giving his body as food, those around him left him, and he turned to his disciples and said, 'Do you want to leave me also?' and Peter said to him, 'Where should we go? Thou hast the word of eternal life.'[60] If you read the Gospel you will see that there is not one passage in the Gospel in which the Lord

---

[60] John 6:68.

describes eternal life. He indicates, here and there, by a word, this is the life of eternity, but he does not use the kind of imagery which we find in mystical literature. What the words of Peter mean is: whenever you speak, your words hit at the very core of our being, like two stones struck together and bringing out a spark. When the core of our being is so affected, eternal life which is dormant in us blossoms out, flares up. This is what the Apostles did, what the early Christians did, because their experience had been a personal experience of meeting the living God face to face. I do not mean meeting Christ in the flesh, I mean that in their experience they knew God through Christ and through the illumined Apostles. When Paul spoke of God he was transfigured, and there is an ancient manuscript, which says that when St Paul was in repose, as it were simply himself, he was as ugly as a devil, but when he spoke of God, he shone with light like an angel of Heaven.

When the Apostles moved from place to place they did not simply change location; they went from place to place with the newness of life which they could impart to others. What about us? Do we impart anything to the people whom we meet, who are around us? What happens to us, to the Christian community, is that with the recognition of Christianity by Constantine and its later spread, the Christian community became secure and sedentary.[61] And these two things are evils. Security means that we do not realise how dangerous are the paths we tread. We do not realise that we are not simply embarked in a ship that will carry us across the ocean of life into eternity. Every step is a challenge. Every step is a danger. Every step is a risk. At every moment evil is before us and God is with us. And we forget too often that the power of God is beyond all the power of evil. Hermas, one of the Seventy, says in one of his epistles: 'Remember, never to fear the power of evil more than your trust in the power and love of God.'[62] So, this is an element which the Apostles could bring to mission, because in the pagan society in which they lived people were terrified of evil, of evil powers, of Satan. And the Apostles came and said, 'Fear not; Christ has conquered. The devil is defeated.

---

[61] The Emperor Constantine ended persecution of the Christians, and made Christianity the official religion of the Empire in the year 313.

[62] *Shepherd of Hermas*: anonymous Christian text dating from the second century which was influential in the Early Church.

If you are with him, you are invincible.' That is not something we often hear today.

The dangers of security

Today, people cling together and do not look outwards, they are afraid of living to the full, of going into the unknown, of meeting face to face those who will reject them, or endanger them. The French preacher Bossuet says, 'How comforting it is to hear that practically in every Church, priests preach on martyrdom. When martyrdom is here one does not speak of it, one endures it. If there is so much talk of martyrdom, it means that we feel secure.'[63] Alas, we feel we are secure. But we are also sedentary in another way. We are encrusted in one place. We have formed Christian communities that are not outward looking. We have services and so many people feel that it is the services that are everything. People come to a service on a Sunday and exclaim, 'If only it was possible not to leave the precincts of this church, because outside there is an alien world', and we forget that Christ said to

---

[63] Jacques-Benigne Bossuet (1627–1704): bishop, theologian and renowned preacher.

us 'Go, like sheep among the wolves, go into the world to make disciples of all nations' (cf. Matt 10:16). This is, as it were, how the Liturgy comes to fruition. If in the Liturgy we have entered into communion with the Holy Spirit and with Christ, then our function is to go out and to bring the glory, the joy and the love of it to others. A mentality has developed among us that we must be secure within the walls of the Church, within the limits of a Christian community. Going out is dangerous, yet that is exactly what we should be doing and we have forgotten it.

It began very early in the Church, the moment we became Christians many things changed. The men and the women who had been prepared to live and to die for Christ were of another stature than the many who joined the Church because the Emperor had joined it. And having entered the Church, they wanted to be secure, but secure under what? Under God? No. Very often under the authority of the imperial power. And at this moment certain things happened: it was the beginning of monasticism. Men of a daring spirit left the cities and the comfort of a state Christianity to go into the wilderness to fight evil in themselves and the evil that was spreading around. Fr Georges Florovsky insists on the fact that these people were not running away from a still pagan society; they were not running away from persecution. They were running away from a Christianity that had 'lost its salt'. They were going away because the Christian community had become devoid of flavour; it was no longer the heroic body it had been in the beginning.

That is the beginning of monasticism, and has been the impetus for it throughout the ages. Even now this should be the attitude of anyone embracing the monastic life. We refuse to accept the anaemic, weak, irresponsible attitude of the sedentary community. We want to be alone with God, and together with God to go into all the situations that need his presence and the giving of our lives. When I speak of giving our lives I do not mean dying; at times, to live a long time in circumstances that are tragic or painful may be more important than to die at once. A Russian bishop, a hero of the years of Soviet persecution of the Church, often said that at times the duty of the believing Christian is to survive. Ever since Cain murdered Abel all the Cains of the world have been trying to murder all the Abels of the world, but the Abels of the world have a function to fulfil and we have learned to survive as long as is necessary for this function to be fulfilled without compromise, allowing God to choose the moment when we will be killed.

At other moments the fools for Christ's sake appeared. They, too, rejected the secure sedentary approach. If you look at the history of the Byzantine Empire, or of Russia, you will discover that the fools for Christ's sake appeared in numbers at a moment when the state, the empire, began to assert its right to build a secure society. At that moment fools for Christ's sake appeared who were an offence to everything that is security. They behaved like fools, while we all treasure our intellect. We want to be safe, to have our intellect working because the intellect cannot be destroyed, otherwise than together with our physical body. But they refused to behave in a socially acceptable manner because the State, and the Church within the State, proclaimed a certain behaviour, a certain way of being and that was no longer acceptable.

Later, we find in Russia and in other countries, pilgrims: people who wandered from one holy place to another, or spent long periods of time in the desert or in the vastness of Russia to be uncompromisingly alone with God and to visit places where they could find a spark of the divine. These people rejected the false security of a sedentary life, because it was a place of ultimate insecurity: their only security, their only safety, was God. And God is totally unsafe and insecure for us when we want to be supported, held, protected. They went into an adventure of ultimate and total risk.

You may ask, what can we do? We cannot all become pilgrims, or fools for Christ's sake, however 'foolish' we may be. It is not a question of what we possess. It is a question of our attitude to our possessions. Possession is a way of being possessed and you may be possessed even by a very small thing. And that is how all of us live to a greater or lesser extent. In the Gospel we find a passage of immense importance, the story of the king calling his closest friends to the bridal feast of his son. One refuses because he has bought a plot of land, the other refuses because he has bought five pairs of oxen, another one refuses because he has just got married.[64] What does this amount to? It means that not only have I bought land, but I think I possess it. I am like a tree which cannot move from the place where it is rooted. I have five pairs of oxen, that is I have something to do in life, and therefore it is more

---

[64] Cf. Matt 22; Luke 14.

important than anything, than friendship, than love, than generosity, than sacrifice. I must do my work. I have married someone, my heart is full, I have no space in my heart for anyone else's joy. And that one is expelled. This is very often our attitude. We have bought a plot of land, we have oxen, we have an attachment, we cannot give our lives to anything that is beyond us and our enslavement. That does not mean that we cannot be free. The question is are you attached or not? There is a difference between love and attachment. You may be the slave of a relationship, or you may be free within it.

And who are the invited? The king sends his servants to bring in the beggars, the lost people who are called to come into the king's presence and they come with a feeling of fear and trembling. At the door they are met by the angels of God, who say to them, 'Come, we will change your clothes, we will bathe your bodies, we will comb your hair and you will then come worthily into the presence of the king.' Only one refuses, saying, 'I was invited to eat, not to bathe, not to be pampered; I want my food.'

This process of attachment has gone deeper into the Church because our liturgical forms have also been penetrated by the effect of our relationship with the State. Our Orthodox Liturgy is deeply influenced by the court ceremonial of Byzantium. In the early Church there was a variety of forms. In Byzantium liturgy had to become worthy of the Emperor and of his court. And so, it was structured in such a way that it could coincide with the forms familiar to the imperial court. The result was the magnificent liturgy that we possess. But it is a mistake to imagine that this is the only form, because in the early centuries there were a number of liturgies that belonged to the same undivided Christian Church. There was the Liturgy of Rome, of St Gregory Dialogus,[65] there was the Liturgy of St Ambrose of Milan, there was the Liturgy of Lyon, there was the Arabic Liturgy, there was the St Germain Liturgy in Paris[66] and a number of others. They were all basically identical because each of them had the same identical core. But they were different in form, in expression, and they corresponded to a freedom which

[65] St Gregory the Great (540–604): Pope of Rome, known in the Eastern Church as St Gregory Dialogus (the Dialoguist) after his writings, *The Dialogues*.

[66] Liturgy ascribed to St Germanus of Paris (496–576), and restored by Fr Evgraph Kovalesky after the foundation of the Orthodox Church of France (an autonomous diocese of Western Rite parishes) in 1936.

very often we have lost, a freedom which corresponded both to the culture of a place and the
social context. We must learn to pray within
the liturgy, to receive from all our services all the
richness it can give, but not to be slaves of it.

The meaning of tradition

I would now like to say a word about the
meaning of tradition. Whenever someone dares
to suggest the slightest change in the ways of the
Church he is accused of breaking with tradition.
And here it is important for us to treasure tradition, but also to understand it rightly and not
to become prisoners and slaves of false tradition.
Tradition is something that is handed down to us
from the very beginning, from one generation to
the other. But what is handed down to us is the
substance and the meaning and not the form. A
Russian bishop in the early years of the emigration wrote that it was not permissible to celebrate
in Western languages because most heresies were
born in the West – forgetting that there were
enough heretics in Byzantium and elsewhere! If
tradition is understood in that sense you become
its prisoner. Tradition is the living memory of the

Church. We all have a memory but more often than not, too often, we forget our past. The Church does not. The Church has an eternal, unshakeable memory. But memory does not mean that nothing new can enter into our experience. This memory does not force us backward at every step. It is an experience that has gradually grown into new and further experience rooted in God and inspired by the Holy Spirit. What the Church does is to look at every step of its development and its life for what St Paul calls 'the mind of Christ'. To listen to the teaching of the Holy Spirit is to be always young, always new, always modern. It does not tell us to live as we lived in the twelfth century.

In a discussion with a group of Russian bishops on the ordination of women, the senior bishop articulated the following conclusion: 'I have no answer on this matter, but it has not happened in the past and therefore it should never happen in the future.' Whether it should happen or not is another matter. But that is not a reason. Tradition is the living memory of almost two thousand years of Christianity, living and kept alive by the action and the inspiration of the Holy Spirit and made solid, unshakeable, by the word and the person of Christ. Traditional*ism* is what a Roman Catholic theologian in America has described as 'the dead memory which is kept by the living':[67] memories of things which do not exist any more in reality, which are totally useless, but which are nonetheless treasured. This is heresy. This denies the fact that the Church is alive. The Shepherd of Hermas speaks in his first vision of meeting a woman of extreme beauty with the face of a virgin and with white hair. He says to her, 'Who are you?' and she answers, 'I am the Church.' 'How is it that you are so young? You have existed for so long.' She replies, 'I have the youth of eternity.' 'But why then have you got white hair?' And the answer came: 'Because I have the hair of wisdom.' And this is what the Church should be. The Church is not a vague, amorphous concept. You, I, we – that is the Church. And we should have the youth of the newly born into eternity, and possess the wisdom of the centuries before us – and even more the wisdom of God that stretches into eternity.

---

[67] Juroslav Pelikan.

The structure of Church and State

A few words on the structure of the Church. The structure of the Church has resulted from copying the structures of the imperial state, which is strictly hierarchical. But according to Fr Sophrony, the State is a pyramid standing on its base, whereas the Church is a pyramid standing on its point. And this point is not a man, not a hierarchy, not a council of bishops. This point is the Lord Jesus Christ, who alone can be the head, the supreme point of the Church, and then, layer after layer of the people who exercise Christ's own *diakonia*, carrying on their shoulders all the weight of the pyramid. If we speak of hierarchy, we must remember Christ's words 'I am in your midst like the servant', and those of us who wish to be in Christ must learn to be servants and nothing else.

However, historically a hierarchy of power has developed; a hierarchy that can command not because what is said is convincing, but because what is said can be enforced. If in the Church we are simply a hierarchy of power because we have different titles and ranks, that is a negation of the very substance and life of the Church. We know how often saints 'of no account' were guides for people who were far above them hierarchically or socially. In the Church power must be replaced by service, by *diakonia*, and as long as we continue to believe in the power of the hierarchy and not in the *diakonia* of the hierarchy, we are not a Church according to the Gospel.

That means that we have to reconsider completely the situation of the laity, the clergy and the episcopate. First of all, deacons appeared some time after Christ's Ascension. They were not ordained by Christ. They were appointed by the disciples, by the Apostles, for a specific function. They do not belong to the original Gospel which we read. Then came the presbyters who took over from the Apostles, then came a seniority of grace and of function. So, it is not out of the Gospel that the hierarchy of the Church sprang. The Church knew only one thing: to be the body of Christ, the temple of the Holy Spirit, the continuation throughout history of the Incarnation and of the voice of the Spirit teaching us to proclaim what Christ has taught us. It is the people of God, as we find in the Epistle, 'a royal priesthood' (1 Pet 2:9), who must make sacred everything they touch, who can sanctify all things by first sanctifying themselves, and then bringing into sanctity everything they touch and do, until God can become 'all in all'. St Basil reminds us that 'anyone can rule, but only a king can give his life for his subjects', and each of us in that respect is endowed with the kingship of Christ, that is, with his command to die for our neighbour and for the salvation of the world. So, this is the laity, the total body of Christ, and within it there are ministries, but they are within it. It is very important to remember that we are all lay people, and bishops are laymen with episcopal grace. We claim to be members of the Body of Christ, and if we are members of it in an individual way, that is to the extent to which we give our lives to others.

A final few words on freedom and faith. We do not know very often what freedom means because we have been taught far too often about the virtue of obedience. Obedience is understood too often in the Church as enslavement, as being submissive, as being ready to be commanded and to obey. But that is not obedience. True obedience is very different. Obedience comes from listening and hearing, and obedience on every level is a school of hearing, not a school of doing what one is told. It is a way of learning from someone who has more experience, something that will allow us to outgrow our own experi-

ence and by learning to renounce our own self-
will, our own prejudices, our own narrow-
mindedness, to expand to the measure of the one
who teaches us; we must learn gradually to
become capable of listening to the voice of the
Holy Spirit within us. And when we read the
Gospel, we must hear not only its words and
commandments, but the voice of truth reaching
us and transforming and transfiguring us. Freedom then ceases to be the opposite of obedience.
The word 'freedom' comes from a Sanskrit word
priyia, which in its verbal form means to love and
to be loved, and as a noun, means 'my beloved'.
Freedom is a relationship of mutual love; of the
gift of self to another, in readiness to listen with
all our mind, all our heart, all our being, and to
love with all our mind, all our heart and all our
being. And if that is true, then it must reach out
into life, into a way of living, because far too
often we imagine that we are Christian or
Orthodox because we proclaim a certain number
of truths which were defined by the Councils or
by 'superior authority' (in very inverted com-
mas). In reality we must learn to receive all that
we are given from the past, and receive it with
newness of heart and mind, with a faith that
expresses itself in every way. Faith is defined as

the certainty of things unseen, but faith is also *faithfulness*, and faith is also a way of living. And so, if we live up to the Gospel with all our courage, with all our energy (and when we have no energy and no courage we turn to God and say 'Lord, fill my weakness with your strength; replace my cowardice with your courage; replace my sloth with your indomitable energy'), then and only then have we the right to say that we are Orthodox. And I will conclude with the words of Pastor Visser't Hooft, the first General Secretary of the World Council of Churches, who said: 'One can be a heretic even while proclaiming every article of the Creed if we give the lie to one or all of them by the way in which we live. One can be a heretic by denying the truth, by not living according to the truth.'[68]

---

[68] Willem A. Visser't Hooft (1900–85) was named General Secretary of the provisional committee of the World Council of Churches at its first meeting in 1938. In 1948 he became General Secretary of the WCC and remained so until his retirement in 1966. Metropolitan Anthony was a member of the WCC Central Committee from 1968 to 1975.

PART V

Eucharist

※ ⁂

The Church as a Eucharistic Community

The following talk, which touches on major issues such as the ordination of women and the place of the Eucharist in the life of the Church, was given to the Twelfth General Assembly of Syndesmos, August 1986, and published in Syndesmos: Report of the Twelfth General Assembly, *17– 24 August 1986 (Joensuu: Syndesmos, 1988), pp. 37–45.*

I do not intend to give a lecture, but to bring to you thoughts that supremely matter to me. The subject which I was given is 'The Church as a Eucharistic Community'. I should like to start by dispelling a misapprehension.

For decades now we have been both prisoners and victims of a eucharistic theology that has resulted in making the Church into a liturgical ghetto, into something extremely small, that is, a self-gathered community – afraid of moving outward. It has thereby prevented us from a wider vision. This notion of the eucharistic community being nothing else, indeed, nothing more, than the gathered community celebrating the eucharistic sacrifice, the Holy Liturgy, has had catastrophic results.

The first is that however great the eucharistic celebration is, it is not the whole worship of the Church. There are many Church communities which have lost, have forgotten, that apart from the Eucharist there is a great variety of prayerful experience within the Church, both liturgical and personal. So many of the Church services in which the Saints have expressed their knowledge of God, through which they have attempted to convey it to us, make us partakers of it, are now discarded in so many parts of the world. Also, and I believe this is even more tragic, there are many who no longer know how to pray except when they are gathered together with others, carried either by a mood or a liturgical sequence, forgetting that the heart of prayer is in the deep silence of the soul, in contemplation, in deep adoration and obedience to God.

There are two further wrongs that result from the liturgical attitude to the eucharistic community. On the one hand there is a false vision of the Church, born of a wrong vision of the act of worship. 'Neopapalism' has grown in the Orthodox Church, because, quite erroneously, some have imagined that the Church of Christ can and should be built as a pyramid: locally a priest celebrating and guiding his flock, then a diocese being headed by a Bishop, a metropolitan area being headed by a Metropolitan Archbishop, and (finally) a local Church, being headed by a Patriarch, or head of Church. The whole thing, ideally, culminating in one person, who would be, as it were, a final icon of Christ, presiding over the universal Liturgy.

This is heresy. There is no other person that can stand at the head of this pyramid but Christ Himself. No one can be the visible head of the Church – no one, ultimately, whether it is in a parish, in a diocese, a metropolitan area, or local Church. No one but Christ is the celebrant of any sacrament. No one, whatever power is vested in him, can command God to enter, actively and creatively, into creatures He has called into existence. No amount of Apostolic Succession can give anyone the power to make this bread into the Body of Christ, or that cup into the Blood of Christ. It is not magic power that we possess over the creatures of God. Indeed, even less do we possess it over God Himself.

The other aspect of this liturgical conception of the gathered community as being all there is to the Church is the structures of oppression. These are structures which result in a hierarchy which is ecclesiastical and clerical and which is totally alien to a sense of the universal priesthood of all believers that is in harmony with a ministerial priesthood. The results are Churches built on a clericalist hierarchy on one side and submissiveness on the other.

The role of women in the Church

A result of this attitude, and the cause of it, is the position of women in the Church. Orthodox have been affirming certain views about the position of women in the Church without ever having given thought to it. Books have been published that are an insult to women and represent extremely poor thinking and theology. We are making assertions which are not based on thought. It has taken centuries for the Church to have a coherent, acceptable and inspiring theology of God – of the relation there is in Him between nature and person, of His energies and personal being, between grace and divinity; of the relation there is between God and His creatures. We should be prepared to realise that we have never given any kind of thought, leaving aside even such words as 'intelligent', or 'creative', to the position and situation of women in the Church.

As long as all there is to the Church is the liturgical celebration, it is easy to see that everyone is equal in a total lack of rights, if he or she is a layperson, and total hegemony if he is a cleric. When it comes to the notion of the universal priesthood of all believers, we discover a form of discrimination completely contrary both to the beginning of Genesis and to the attitude of Christ, which we can deduce from the Gospels. And when we try to give a *ratio*, a *rationale*, for these things, we are told they have no *rationale* – except tradition. Perhaps we should remember the words of the American theologian Pelikan, who said: 'Tradition is the living memory of the Church throughout the ages: Traditionalism is the dead adherence of contemporaries to what they imagine were the convictions, or faith, of their ancestors.'[69] We must rethink the problems of femininity, of

---

[69] Professor Jaroslav Jan Pelikan (1923–2006): Church historian, and author of *The Christian Tradition* (1971–89: five volumes) in which he pointed out the difference between tradition and traditionalism.

womanhood and manhood, with the same earnestness we have thought out the problems of nature and person in God, of grace and nature, and so forth. And short of this we have no right to express, with the arrogance we have exhibited in the last few decades, views which I hope one day will be rejected by the whole Church.

To refer us, for example, to the person of the Mother of God, and tell women that they should follow her example and be as inconspicuous as possible, is slander against the Mother of God. It is extremely poor vision. We see in the Mother of God something very different. She is not an instrument of the Incarnation. She is as totally active in it as God Himself. Saint Gregory Palamas says, 'Without the assent of the Mother of God, the Incarnation would have been as impossible as it would have been without the positive Will of God the Father.'

We see in the ministry of all believers that every Christian is called to bring himself, soul and body, as a living sacrifice to God. And I remind you that the word 'sacrifice' does not simply mean a blood offering, or even an offering, but an act by which something that was either profane, or profaned, becomes sacred and holy, with the Holiness of God Himself.

When we think of the ministerial office, we see that that office consists in the fact that it is not only himself that the priest brings forth to God as an offering. All the Church performs is the sacrifice by the hands and voice of the priest. It is Christ's own life and death, His descent into hell, His Resurrection, His glorious Ascension, which are brought forth before the eyes of God and before the eyes of all people.

If we think of the Mother of God, tradition tells us that she was brought up into the Holy of Holies, into which the High Priest alone was allowed to enter, and this only once a year, and not otherwise than after ritual purification by blood. She, more than anyone, has brought forth the blood offering which is the sacrifice of Christ. She did this first when she brought her divine Son to the Temple to be offered to God, in accordance with the Law. And she did so when she stood silent, without a word of protest, without a cry for mercy, by the Cross which brought about the death of her Son for the salvation of the world. These thoughts I want to leave with you in the context of these structures which are born of our narrow, at times heretical, and certainly traditionalist views of the situation of men and women, and of the Eucharist within the life of the Church.

The mystery of the Church

But does this mean that the Eucharist is secondary? Does what I said mean that I do not revere the Holy Sacrament as it should be revered? No. I can say in all honesty, that I approach both Communion and the celebrating of the mysteries with all the devotion, all the brokenheartedness, and all the love of which I am capable. But we must remember the words of Khomiakov in the nineteenth century, that the Church is greater than any of its sacraments. The Church contains them all. He says, 'The Church is the only sacrament, the only mystery, of the world.' Those of you who know Greek need no explanation, and those of you who do not know Greek may well remember that the word 'mystery' does not mean something which is mysterious, but something with which we are confronted in awe, in sacred terror, and which makes us spellbound, mute, silent, so that we have no word, no gesture, to offer; so that we stand in sacred awe and adoration. We can know what it conveys only by sharing what is offered to our experience.

May I remind those of you who are not familiar with the 'secret' prayers of the Orthodox

Liturgy,[70] that after Communion, and before he transfers the Holy Gifts from the altar to the table of preparation, the Priest asks God 'to grant that we may commune ever more truly' with Himself than we have done by communicating in the Holy Body and Blood of Christ in the sacramental communion. This he does partly because the liturgy on earth has an eschatological quality – all is given but not all is received. We are too small to contain the greatness of what is given. But, partly, because we are called to a communion with God so infinitely profound that nothing can be the end of it. We are, to use a phrase of Saint Maximus the Confessor, 'to unfold the limitless limits of infinity'. Or, to take a quotation from the Scripture, 'We are called to be partakers of the Divine Nature' (1 Pet 2:9). We are to live by all that is God's own life.

In this context I should like to say a word about what the Church is, and how the sacraments, and particularly the eucharistic sacrament, relate to the Church and to us. The Church

---

[70] The 'secret prayers' are those designated to be said in a low voice by the priest, and are not audible outside the sanctuary. However, many of these prayers – particularly those at the heart of the Eucharist – are said aloud in contemporary practice.

is a body which is both, simultaneously, equally, human and divine. In the Person of Christ, true man, Jesus of Nazareth, of whom Saint Paul speaks, we have a revelation of what true humanity should be, is called to become, and indeed shall be, by the power and grace of God. And in Him we see that no one is truly and perfectly human who is not a partaker of the life of God, who is not one with God, in whom God does not live freely.

On the other hand, humanity is represented in the Church by us who are sinful, and yet united with Christ, and God, by faith, and by the sacraments. We are men and women in becoming, in the process of becoming what we are called to be – the children of God. 'Children' is a vague word. We are called to be, with regard to the Father all that Christ is. Saint Ireneaus of Lyon teaches us that in Christ, by the Power of the Holy Spirit, each of us and the sum total of humanity, is called to become the Only-Begotten Son of God. We enter into this relationship by adoption. But we do not remain always, as happens in human families, only adopted, that is distinct from the natural child. In Him we become what He is.

The Holy Spirit is also alive, abroad, and

acting within the Church. Acting as powerfully, pervading all things, calling us, unfolding before us, the understanding of what God has said in and through Christ, revealing to us meaning which humanly speaking in our fallen humanity, we are incapable of perceiving. He is also our counsellor. Because if we truly love Christ the fact of not being at one with Him already now, of communing with Him incessantly, the fact that we are separated from Him until we die, should provoke in us acute and constant pain and longing – the same pain which we feel when we are separated from the person we love above all others on earth. And that should lead us to a true attitude to death – a longing for death, not understood as losing our temporary ephemeral life, but as being vested with eternity so that we can meet Christ and God face to face and know Him as we are known by Him. Saint Paul expresses this by saying 'I no longer live, it is Christ who lives within me.' He longs to die – because as long as he is in the flesh he is separated from Christ. But his culminating word at that point – and it is essential for our purpose, is that he says, 'and yet it is expedient for you that I should live'. And I shall. I shall accept separation from God for as long as necessary because I must be in your midst His witness and herald, His proclaimer, His apostle.

If you remember the words of Saint Ireneaus which I have quoted, if you remember the words of Saint Paul, 'Our life is hid with Christ in God', you will realise that Christ is a door: He opens to us access to the Father. The whole Trinitarian Mystery resides within the Church, together with all human mystery. There is indeed such a thing as the human mystery. To see in Christ, in the saints, that man is deep and vast enough not only to contain God, but to commune with Him, to become a partaker of His very nature, is a revelation of a greatness in man which no degree of arrogance or pride could suggest. We are called to be as great as Him. You will remember the words of Angelus of Silesius, a mystic of the Rhine, who said, 'I am as great as God; he is as small as I.' We should try to reflect on that, and, perhaps, project this thought onto the problems of men, women and children and ministries, and so on.

The place where God and man are united

The Church is a place where men and God are united. More than this, the Incarnation is not simply a way in which God united Himself to mankind. The Word became flesh. The Divinity of Christ pervaded His human body as totally and perfectly as it filled His soul, and His humanity. That is why we believe that in the tomb the body of Christ was incorruptible: because it was inseparable from His Divinity. In Him this body of Christ; was filled with Divinity in the same way in which the bread and wine are filled with His Divinity and Presence. This body stands as an image of the whole cosmos, because it is the same physical material that makes the cosmos, that makes our bodies. In Him the whole cosmos could recognise itself glorified and brought to its fulfilment, a revelation of what things will be, when, according to Saint Paul, 'God will be all in all'. God will be not only present in us, not uniting us alone, but all creatures will be infused with the Divine Presence. This is the vision of the Church.

If such is our situation then, the Church contains the Eucharist – even if the Eucharist is an

absolutely decisive vision of eschatological fulfilment. But a vision is like a prophecy. It is a
beginning. It has an incipient quality. But it is
not yet the thing unfolded, fully deployed.

The sacraments of initiation

Let me now say something about the three
sacraments of initiation which are essential:
baptism, the gift of the Holy Spirit in chrismation and the Eucharist, the first moment when we
become partakers of the Holy Body and Blood of
Christ given us sacramentally.

Baptism is death and resurrection. As we see it
in the Church, the descent into the baptismal
font is a drowning. It represents for us a dying,
but a dying which is peculiar because the waters
of baptism in this baptismal font are not simply a
river, a sea, into which we fall in order to lose our
temporary lives. It is Christ into whom we are
plunged. What is to die in us is all that is alien to
Christ: not our temporary life, but all that sin has
made it. We are plunged into what St Paul calls
the 'death of Christ' (Rom 6:3), and we must
emerge out of the baptismal font possessed of the
death of Christ, having died to all that is alien to

God, all that is unworthy of Him and unworthy of us as true human beings.

An analogy may help. You remember how often Christ performs a miracle of healing? What happens? Before He came into the presence of the sufferer the mortal life which we inherited from our ancestors, this mortal life was gradually waning – like blood running out of a wound, so that its end is death. Christ restores health. But He does not say to us: 'You are back where you were and you can start living in the same sinful and destructive manner in which you lived before.' What He says to us is: 'All that was your natural life has brought you to a premature death. The life which I am giving you now is a new life. It is not yours. It is a life of grace. It is my life, which I share with you. And I can do this because, on Calvary, I share with you your death.' So when we rise again from the baptismal font we rise possessed of the death of Christ in order to be possessed of the life of Christ, not of our own life. No longer do I live, it is Christ that lives in me. It is categorical, as categorical as this.

Then the Holy Spirit is poured into us, and upon us, and we are sealed as vessels that contain this Divine Presence. This is a fulfilment of our restored, renewed humanity. We are not in a position to move back to the condition of Adam and Eve before the Fall. Yet we become miraculously, eschatologically, partakers of something which will be when time is over, and God's victory is won – won over us, over Satan, over all things that are separated from God. It is because we are dead to the world, alive with the Life of Christ, possessed of the Holy Spirit in the same terms that Christ, before baptism, received the descent of the Holy Spirit in His humanity, that we can approach the Holy Sacrament of the Body and Blood of Christ. It is because we are in communion that we can receive Communion especially on that one and first occasion when we are in communion and receive Communion in a way that is unrepeatable and unique – because we have never before communed with Christ the way we have at that moment.

Saint Justin[71] says something that we should ponder. What matters is this first Communion, which together with baptism, and the gift of the Holy Spirit in the laying on of hands, or chrismation, makes us into Christians, into members of the Body of Christ. He says that this could be enough for life. If we did not allow it to wax old,

---

[71] Justin Martyr.

to lose the grace received, if we could keep it contained and make what we are given on this first occasion bear fruit, we would need no longer to repeat the act of Communion. At this point it is right to say that attitudes may differ. In a sort of absolute theological sense, however, it may be enough – for this first Communion has made us into Christ's members.

On the other hand, we may receive sacramental Communion again and again because we are in communion. Then we become partakers of the Banquet of the Lamb, a banquet that does not repeat itself, but continues day after day, hour after hour, without ceasing, in a miracle of rejoicing together.

We know that some saints felt that they could not receive Communion more than very seldom because they felt they would break under the weight of it, explode. It is said that the teacher of Saint Joseph of Volokolamsk,[72] Paphnutis Borovsky, having been asked to celebrate the liturgy in a monastery because there was no priest available, said afterwards, 'Don't ever ask me to do it again. A man cannot face or perceive what I have perceived, and live.'

---

[72] St Joseph of Volokolamsk (1439–1515): abbot, theologian and monastic reformer.

Between these extremes the wisdom of the Church teaches us that all nuances are possible. We can come in a variety of situations and moods. But we must always remember that Communion, like God, is a devouring fire and that it is a dreadful thing to fall into the hands of the Living God if we cannot commune with Him, that is, unite with Him on His terms.

I always say to priests who will be ordained: 'Remember, that in the service in the preparation, when you will prepare the lamb of sacrifice, and cut it crossways, saying "the Lamb of God is divided and sacrificed", if you do not unite yourself to His sacrifice with all your faith, all your will, all your readiness to live and die the life of Christ, you are not the celebrant, you are one of the murderers who crucified Him.'[73] That is applicable to everyone who is present at the liturgy. The priest is not the only celebrant, it is the whole Church. And so we are confronted, all of us, with this responsibility when we receive this Body and Blood.

If we think in these terms then we will see what the liturgical community is. The liturgical

---

[73] During the Proskomedia, or Liturgy of Preparation, the priest cuts the loaf crosswise, saying, 'Sacrificed is the Lamb of God ...'

community, the Eucharist event, is a moment when we become partakers in Christ in a final, total and ultimate way. But then we must enter the life which is ours on Christ's own terms – all that was true of Him as a Priest, Prophet and King must be true of us. He came into the world to save the world. He became a partaker of all its problems, sufferings, everything. And we are all called to enter this world but not as a gathered community. This is a joy which is given to us once a week, or less, according to circumstances. It is a moment when we are renewed, when we commune with Christ in order to be His. He says, 'Those who love me will fulfil my commandments' (cf. John 14:15). He does not say, 'Those who love me will forget all the world, all its needs, all its sufferings, all the reasons why I have become man, in order to cling to me and rejoice in the liturgical celebration and in the pleasures of liturgical music, or the joy of human fellowship.'

We are sent out into the world

In that moment of communion, we must receive something that will send us in all directions as the Apostles were sent. The word 'apostle' means 'one who is sent'. We are not simply sent to look at our close neighbours. We are sent to those who are lost. To be a eucharistic community does not mean to be the gathered liturgical community, self-sufficient. It consists in being the Body of Christ, an extension of His incarnate presence in the world: active, sharing with the whole world the exultant joy of what we have discovered, a God who loves us so much that He accepts to become man, to become vulnerable, to become helpless, to be seemingly defeated, to suffer, to be betrayed, to be renounced, mis-understood, judged, condemned, crucified, laid in a tomb, to descend into the hell of perdition. We must be everywhere Christ would have been. Where there is darkness, we must be there. If we are His presence, His words 'I am the Light of the World' (John 9:5) must apply to us. We must go into the darkness of the world, into the twi-light of the world. Where there is suffering, we must be there – and be Christ's compassion. Where there is sin, we must be there – and be the salt of the earth that saves it from corruption. Where there is evil, we must take it into ourselves – and fight it, and overcome it. In Christ, humanity and divinity were united so that the conflict became internal to Him, and resolved in Him. We must do the same. One could go on giving examples. But you must understand that our place is not where it is safe, our place is where things are evil, where things need salvation – not where things are in no need of any such presence.

Now I would like to end in the few minutes left to me, by something which is relevant to you as young people. We should all learn to be younger and younger. I had a quotation presented to me a few days ago: 'We are all born old. We must live in such a way that we die young.' We are all born old. We have the weight of our ancestry. Once we are born, and while still young children, our parents, our contemporaries, our teachers, our very *milieu*, load us with more and more of this weight. The problem of life is, like a butterfly who gets freed from a cocoon, gradually to get free from this age-long wait and to fly out young. This is something which is a problem for the old, but it is also a problem for you. For one does not do that at the end of one's life. It is not of a sudden that you can tear the cocoon and fly. It is a lifelong effort to break through all this cramping load of the past and present, and become alive with eternity.

You may remember this passage from Victor Hugo's poem 'Boaz Asleep'. Speaking of Boaz in old age, he says: 'The old man, who is returning to the primeval source of light, enters into days eternal and moves out of temporary things. And one can see fire in the eyes of the young, but one sees light in the eyes of the old.' This is the way of Christ. We must all learn to become young, and be a light to the world, in the context of this rich, wonderful reality which is the Church.

12

❄❦

Vanguard of the Kingdom

*The following talk was given at Pushkin House, London,
on 4 March 1988.*

Some years ago, Archbishop Alexis van der
Mensbrugghe said to me: 'I can't understand
how it is: I am a learned theologian and I need a
lot of preparation before I give a talk. You know
nothing and you are always prepared to talk.'
And he left the question open. Well, this is the
situation at present. I want to say something
about the Church as a eucharistic community,
because it is a term which is very widely used
and which I believe is fraught with great risks
and leading to great misunderstandings. Partly
because of the growth of the practice of frequent
Communion in the parishes, the term of 'eucharistic community' has come to mean in the

minds of most people that the Church can be defined as the gathered community around the eucharistic celebration. And up to a point this is true. The Church is the only body in the world that is possessed of this mystery of communion of our mystical union with Christ through his Body and Blood. But this conception of the Church as a gathered community, and more especially as a community centred on one of the sacraments of the Church, has, to my mind, serious consequences and very unsatisfactory ones.

One thing is that the Church cannot be defined by any one or even by the sum total of all its sacraments. What happens in the Church is a face-to-face encounter between the Living God and living souls. What happens is the dynamic action of the Living God transforming and transfiguring human beings into beings that belong simultaneously to the earth and to heaven, to time and to eternity.

If we want to understand what the Church is in its nature and essence, we must realise that the Church is a body simultaneously and equally human and divine. And the same way in which the Gospel teaches us that the fullness of the Godhead was present in the flesh in Christ, in the same way the plenitude of God is present in the Church. The Church is human in us. It is also human in our Lord Jesus Christ, in a different way and yet in a similar manner. In us the Church is human as a body of people who have given themselves to God and whom God has received.

St Ephraim of Syria defines the Church as the crowd of repentant sinners – sinners indeed, but repentant in the true sense of the word, not bewailing their sinfulness, but sinners who have turned away from themselves, from all that is alien to God, whose gaze is fixed on the Living God and who are moving Godward. In us the Church is made of sinners but not of sinners orphaned in the world, abandoned of God, estranged from Him, but of sinners who are accepted by God as His children. And in Christ, true God but also true man, we can see what man is in the fullness of this word, because to be true man means to be perfectly, truly human and perfectly united with God. It is only in our unity with God that we acquire our true and full human quality. We are all subhuman, to the extent that we are separated from God to a greater or lesser degree, by intention, by sin, by slackness or forgetfulness.

And so within the Church we can see two things. We can see true, perfect, fulfilled humanity in the Son of God who has become the Son of Man, in whom the fullness of God abides in the flesh, and we can see humanity in us, humanity in the making, a humanity which we should not really call humanity and confuse it with what our vocation is, with what human nature is called to be. And then Christ is not only true man and perfect man. He is God come into the world, the Word that has taken flesh, the Living God in our midst, Emmanuel, our Saviour, Jesus.

And so even on this level of humanity through the presence of Christ, inalienable from us, who is one of us – does He not say to the women after His resurrection: 'Go and tell Peter and my brothers' (cf. Matt 28:10)? Yes, His brothers we are, and His sisters in humanity. The fullness of God is present, but not only in and through Christ. The Holy Spirit was given to the Church, and each of us becomes the dwelling-place of the Holy Spirit through chrismation, through this extension of the gift of Pentecost throughout the ages.

And again we are not simply temples of the Holy Spirit. The presence of the Holy Spirit in us is not simply an indwelling which might give us a sense that He and us are separate, that we are, as it were, only a vessel containing His presence. He pervades us like fire pervades iron, like warmth pervades a human body. He pervades us in spirit, in soul and in the flesh, singly, and He lives and acts with sovereignty within the Church.

And again if we are the sons and daughters of the Living God, the fullness of God with the totality of humanity, this is the Church: a body, an organism equally, simultaneously fully human and divine in the making in each of us, already fulfilled in Christ, already revealed as victory in the Mother of God and in the saints. If that is the Church as seen by Khomyakov as I have tried to present it, then is it not obvious that one cannot reduce the Church to one situation, even to the gathered community participating in the holiest meal one can conceive, because all and everything in the Church is communion with God, and all and everything in the Church is God at work, calling, saving, transforming, transfiguring each of us – and not only this but also sending us into the world. This is another dimension of the Church which we ignore too easily because it is so easy to be the gathered community rejoicing in one another, participating in the gifts of God and separated from the rest.

St Paul says – and I am using a translation of Dr Moffatt in his rendering of St Paul's epistles – the Church is the vanguard of the Kingdom. We are people whose mother country is God's Kingdom. We are in the world, yet not of the world if we are aware of who and what we are, and we are sent to conquer this world for God to make it into the Kingdom of God. But here again I believe we should nuance the notion of this conquest. Secular armies, kingdoms, countries, nations conquer one another and by doing this they subdue those who have been conquered. The role of the Church, of this vanguard of the Kingdom, is to penetrate into the world that is fallen away from its fullness and from God and to set it free. We are called to enter the world which is now alien to God in order to free it from all the fetters that make it a prisoner of death, of sin, of evil, of Satan. We are a liberating army. But again, as St Paul puts it, our role is that of the soldier, and a soldier must be prepared to shed his blood and to die in the service of his king and in the fulfilling of his duty. And this we can see throughout history in the missionaries that gave their lives to proclaim the Gospel, who were not only preachers of the Gospel, but the very message of the Gospel incarnate in persons.

The supreme missionary is perhaps St John the Baptist, of whom St Mark's Gospel, repeating the words of Isaiah, says: 'a voice shouting in the desert' (Mark 1:3). This is not merely a man that shouts the words of God. He is God's voice mediated by a human being. He is the message. There is nothing in him which is not the message. Nothing is left in him but that. And that is what we should learn. And when in our Churches we try to develop a spirit of community, to be the gathered community and rejoice in our closeness and in our participation in the divine mysteries, if that is all we do, we betray our essential function: we are not what we are called to be.

The Church is sent into the world to sanctify it, to make it holy, to make of it the first fruits of the Kingdom that will come, when the Lord will come again and reign supreme. In that context I want to go back to the expression 'eucharistic community'. It is the word 'eucharistic' that so often beguiles us, because the word Eucharist has come to mean for us that particular celebration of the Last Supper of the Lord. But the Greek word and its Slavonic renderings cover a much wider range of notions. I will think in Slavonic terms because as Archbishop Alexis pointed out, my knowledge is very limited; I feel safer. And the word *blagodat* in Old Slavonic means more than one thing. It means a good gift, a supremely good gift. And this supremely good gift is the gift of God to us. It is the gift of the life, the death and the resurrection and the ascension of Christ. It is the gift of Himself creating the Church as I have tried to describe it. It also means gratitude in Slavonic. Indeed, you probably remember the psalm in which King David says: 'How shall I reward God for all that He has given me?' And the answer is: 'I shall take the cup of salvation. I will sing His praises in His courts' (Ps 116:12–13). The first move of gratitude consists in accepting, receiving wholeheartedly, with a rejoicing heart, the gift of love which is given, which is offered. This is the first move of gratitude, not a word or a prayer of thanksgiving, but the sense of marvel, what the French would call *emerveillement*, the sense of 'Oh, to be loved in this way, oh the joy of it, all the wonder of it' – that is where gratitude begins.

And then it must overflow like the cup of which the psalms speak. It must overflow in being to God all that we can be, to live in such a way that we should be a joy to Him, to be such people that He could rejoice in us, feel happy that He gave His life and His death and His message to us. I was about to say 'console the Lord for His crucifixion by showing that He did not die in vain', rejoice Him by the fruits which His life and death and resurrection and ascension has brought to us. So the Church is the place of the supreme gift of God to us, and everything that goes with it – the sacraments indeed, and prayer, and our sonship and the condition of being daughters of God and brothers and sisters of one another and so on. But this exultation of gratitude must break up the gathered community and send us into the world, not with a theoretical message collected or learned by heart in the Gospel or in other parts of the Scriptures, no, with a message received, a message that has made us into living beings from corpses that we were, as in C. S. Lewis's image of statues transformed. We must share with others something that is of a supreme importance to us, that has made all the difference to what we are, what we live for, what we long for. We should be people who are so entranced by our encounter with God, by our integration into this mysterious body which is the Church, that we should be unable to keep our peace. We should be bubbling over with this experience in the way in which we do bubble over when we have read a book that has entranced us, seen a film, heard a concert or met a person and turned to everyone saying, 'Have you read it, have you seen it, have you met him or her?' Are we like this? Then there would be no such thing as Sunday Christians and then a whole week of drab existence, because it is in the week that we would be the Christians that we are to be. Coming to church, praying together would be a joy unutterable, communion with God through prayer and sacrament would be a new life poured into us. But this life should overflow and reach everyone whom we meet, not in the form of pious discourse, but in the shining of a life which is an act of gratitude to God, an effort, a longing to make Him rejoice in His death upon the cross because of the fruits it has borne.

So that would indeed be the Church understood as eucharistic community, but not the kind of eucharistic community of which one speaks all the time and which is a community gathered upon itself, forgetful of the fact that the whole world is dying and that we are called to be the messengers of Christ, the salt that prevents corruption, the light that dispels darkness. And you could find so many other images in the Old and the New Testament, and indeed so many examples in the life of the Church throughout the centuries of people who have been all these things.

The gathered community

And now I want to go back for a moment to this eucharistic community as we think of it all too often, as the gathered community and its structures. The community is gathered, as we see it, around the Eucharist, which is only – I repeat it – only one of the sacraments of the Church but not the whole of it. One does not become a Christian through the Eucharist but through Baptism. One does not receive the Holy Spirit through the Eucharist but through the extension of the gift of Pentecost. One does not enter into marriage through the Eucharist alone, and so forth.

But there is more to it. Those who have made the eucharistic celebration into the pattern of the Church have been instrumental in creating a Church which is false in its structures, a church which is built hierarchically according to liturgical schemes. No one is a celebrant of any of the sacraments but the Lord Jesus Christ. No one can fulfil, perform a sacrament otherwise than the Holy Spirit. No apostolic succession, no ordination, no consecration can give a human being power to take the bread and the wine, creatures of God, free from human enslavement, and force them to become the Body of Christ and the Blood of Christ. And no one by dint of any ordination or consecration can force God into the bread of the Eucharist or into the wine of the Chalice. And this is a statement which I know is hard and which I am prepared to support.

But the danger of this eucharistic, liturgical structuring of a theology of the Church results in structures of power, structures of submission and enslavement. And this is exactly the contrary of what the Church is called to be. I told you earlier that the vocation of the Church is to be a body of people that sets the created world free from all forms of enslavement. The Church knows nothing about power. God in Christ has never been a manifestation of power but of authority. And the difference is important. Power means the ability to force people to do or to say or to act in one way or another. Authority is the ability of a person, through example, through the shining of personality, through words that convey meaning and life, to change the attitude of people.

You remember how, when Christ spoke to the

crowd, a number of His listeners turned away and went. And Christ said to His disciples: 'Are you also going to leave me?' And Peter said to Him: 'Where should we go? Thou hast the words of eternal life' (John 6:68). These were not words by which Christ described eternal life. There is not one passage in the Gospel in which eternal life is described. It is not a way in which He called people into eternal life. It was words which reached people at the very core of their being and awakened eternity in them, made them partakers of eternal life now, not in any kind of mechanical, even sacramental way, but by calling out of the human chaos the image of God and the divine quality of man.

And so it is important for us to free ourselves from this imagery of the eucharistic community built as a liturgical function that may be small in a parish, vaster in a diocese, far too big in a patriarchate, and ultimately a betrayal of its very idea if we think of the Church universal with one head that represents Christ. No one represents Christ. Christ is the only Head of the Church, the only Shepherd, the only Lord, the only Saviour.

And if you look further [you see] the structures of oppression which this causes: yes indeed, one can speak of structures of oppression in the

Church, because when you look at the Church – and I am speaking of the Orthodox Church but I believe it applies perfectly well to all human bodies, Church or not – you see power at work, the superior overpowering the inferior. And the inferior is inferior only in the hierarchical scheme, not because he is spiritually less, not because he is unworthy, not because he is not a saint, but because he does not occupy a hier- archical situation. Orders can be given. Orders must be fulfilled. There is far too much readiness on the part of the laity to be bleating sheep and never confront their parish priest or their bishop with things which are true. I do not mean they should insult them, but should tell them in a brotherly way. I tried to do that once in the army without much success. We had a young lieu- tenant who imagined that he was in command of everything, and he was the object of universal ridicule. I felt terribly sorry for him, so I went to his office, knocked at the door, stood at atten- tion, and he said 'Forward' so I marched and stood still, and he said, 'What have you got to say?' I said to him, 'I want to tell you that you are making a fool of yourself and everyone knows that you are one by the way in which you behave.' He looked at me and said, 'Get out of here before you are under arrest.' But the thing is that a bishop or a priest cannot put you under arrest. So in that sense you are safe. On the other hand – and that I think is important – anyone in the Church has a right to be helped not to be in the wrong. Anyone including the patriarch has a right to be told, 'Look, what you are doing is a mistake. What you are trying to be is a caricature of what you are as a person and the beauty of Christ's image in you.' We all have a right to be helped.

And then there is the universal priesthood of the laity. And if you reflect on what this universal priesthood is, you may easily realize that the function of the priest is to detach from the fallen and distorted world in which we live what can be detached, brought back to God and sanctified. When we perform sacraments, we take a piece of bread and a cup of wine that were born in the monstrosity of the fallen world, but we take it and bring it back to God. They become His own through an act of faith of ours, because we are His own and it is our function to do this. And we bring it as an offering. And we bring upon everything which we can bring to him – human relationship, love, objects which we bless, and so on, his divine grace, making them already in this fallen world to partake of the ultimate victory of the Kingdom. They are already of the Kingdom and they can convey to us what we can no longer possess because we are fallen. So the universal vocation of the Christian is to bring back to God, in all the walks of life which are his what is of this world and sanctify it. As far as we are concerned, we must – to use the words of the Prayer Book – bring to God as a perfect offering our souls and bodies, our whole selves to be His, and through that everything which we touch can be sacred or made sacred or left to be secular; in other words profaned, because there is nothing which is profane by nature.

And then on another level, there is the fact that we have forgotten, in practice (I am not speaking of theologians who write about it but of the reality of the Church) what the universal priesthood of the laity is. A priest is a layman in clerical orders, but a lay person has got a sacred function, because all Christians by vocation are people who must sanctify, make holy the world in which we live and transform it into a city of man that is vast, deep and holy enough for its first citizen to be called Jesus, the Son of God become the Son of Man.

That will explain to you what I mean by

eucharistic community. It is indeed the gathered community, but a community that explodes into being the vanguard of the Kingdom, the scattered community being almost more essential than the gathered one. If you remember the words, for instance, of St Justin Martyr, who said that it could be enough for a Christian to be baptised, receive the gift of the Holy Spirit and Communion once in his life, it could be enough, because the gifts of God cannot be taken away, and what is given once is ours for ever. So if we were deprived of Communion throughout our lives, we might be deprived of a joy, but not of our oneness with Christ. So we could receive Communion once and go into the world, as so many martyrs have done, as so many missionaries have done in olden times. And unless we recapture this dimension, we betray the world, we betray God, we make useless the Incarnation and the death of Christ and His Resurrection.